I0178335

RESTRICTED

HUGHES HK-1 (H-4) FLYING BOAT MANUAL

HUGHES TOOL COMPANY
AIRCRAFT DIVISION

Please note: due to the age and rarity of this manual, some content may be substandard.

ISBN #978-1-935327-78-3 1-935327-78-X

INTRODUCTION

The primary function of this manual is to describe the aircraft, its equipment, its operation, and its characteristics in such detail that the information provided will be sufficient for a flight crew to intelligently, safely, and efficiently accomplish a complete flight. The manual is divided into eight sections and an appendix as follows:

SECTION I, DESCRIPTION - A general picture of the complete airplane describing what is in the airplane and where it is located. This section is reserved primarily for brief descriptive material and therefore does not contain detailed information, system management, or flight operating instructions.

SECTION II, NORMAL OPERATING INSTRUCTIONS - CHECK LISTS - An amplified check list covering any normal flight.

SECTION III, EMERGENCY OPERATING INSTRUCTIONS - Clearly and concisely describes the procedure to be followed in meeting any emergency (except those in connection with the auxiliary equipment) that could reasonably be expected to be encountered.

SECTION IV, AUXILIARY EQUIPMENT - Description, normal operation, and emergency operation of all equipment not actually essential to the airplane's flight, such as communication equipment, automatic pilot, and combustible gas alarm equipment.

SECTION V, OPERATING LIMITATIONS - Covers all important limitations that must be observed during normal operation.

SECTION VI, PERFORMANCE CHARACTERISTICS - A discussion of the general flight characteristics of the airplane summarizing all important flight characteristics which place it at an advantage or disadvantage.

SECTION VII, SYSTEMS DESCRIPTION AND OPERATION - Detailed description and discussion of the operation of the various aircraft systems emphasizing special problems that must be considered in the operation of these systems.

SECTION VIII, CREW DUTIES - An amplified check list covering the complete pre-flight inspection to be accomplished by the first and second flight engineer.

APPENDIX I, OPERATING DATA - Contains operating data charts necessary for preflight and inflight mission planning and explanations on the use of data presented.

TABLE OF CONTENTS

SECTION I - DESCRIPTION

SECTION II - NORMAL OPERATING INSTRUCTIONS - CHECK LISTS

TABLE OF CONTENTS

TABLE OF CONTENTS

SECTION I - DESCRIPTION

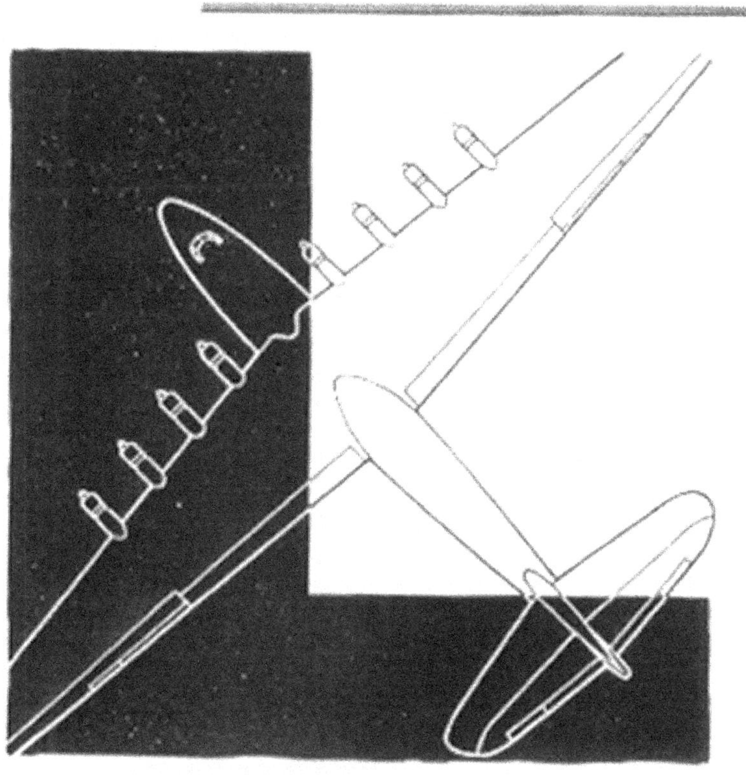

TABLE OF CONTENTS

SECTION 1 - DESCRIPTION

TABLE OF CONTENTS

TABLE OF CONTENTS

SECTION I - DESCRIPTION

1-1 THE AIRPLANE -

1-1.1 General - The Hughes Flying Boat is a cargo type airplane having eight Pratt and Whitney R4360-4A engines, single vertical tail, fixed wing tip floats, and full cantilever wing and tail surfaces. Its structure and surface are entirely of laminated wood; all primary control surfaces except the flaps are fabric covered. Contained in the hull are a flight deck for the operating crew and a large cargo deck with a circular stairway providing access from one deck to the other. Below the cargo deck are located the fuel bays separated by watertight bulkheads. Basic crew personnel are listed in Chapter 5-1. Beaching of the airplane is accomplished by the use of dry dock facilities.

1-1.2 Dimensions - (See Fig. ________)

(a) Wing and Empennage -

	Wing	Horizontal Tail	Vertical Tail
Area (sq ft)	11,430	2610.1	1703.443
Span (ft)	319.92	113.5	49.5
Mean Aerodynamic chord (ft)	38.13	24.681	38.231
Root chord (ft)	51.7	31.13	53.167
Tip chord (ft)	19.65	16.808	17.144
Root section	NACA 63,(420) 321, (a = 1)	NACA 0012-64 (modified) to 10.714% thickness	
Tip section	NACA 65,(318) 415, (a = 1)	NACA 0012-64 (modified) to 10.714% thickness	
Geometric twist (degrees)	4°	0°	0°
Aspect ratio	9.0	4.94	1.438
Taper ratio	0.378	0.5399	0.322
Incidence with fuselage reference line (degrees)	+5° (root chord)	+1°	0°
Dihedral (degrees)	3-1/2°	0°	0°

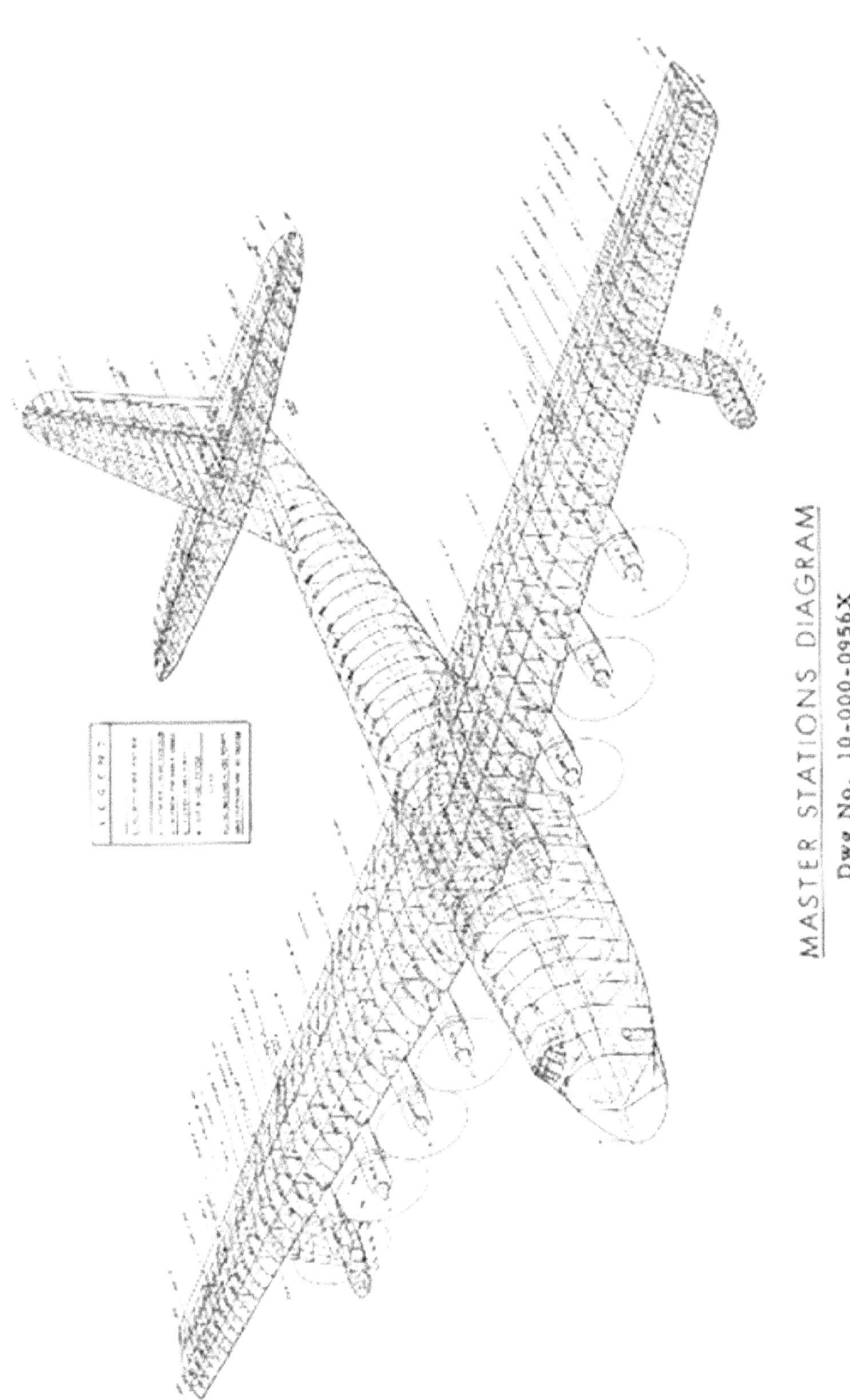

MASTER STATIONS DIAGRAM
Dwg No. 10-000-0956X

(b) Control Surfaces -

	Flaps	Elevators (both)	Rudder	Ailerons (both)
Total area (sq ft)	1404	1110.2	650.56	1250
Area aft of hinge line (sq ft) . .		832.8	477.924	780
Span (ft)		104.318	47.661	143.5
Span (% wing span)	46.0			
Average chord aft of hinge line (ft) .		7.98	10.0	5.45
Chord (% surface chord)	22.84	34.2	28.3	20
Control travel (degrees)	45°	15° down 25° up	20° L & R	12° down 18° up
Type of nose balance		Overhang	Overhang	Internal Seal

(c) Flying Tabs -

	Elevator Flying Tabs	Rudder Flying Tabs	Aileron Flying Tabs
Area aft of hinge line (sq ft) . .	90.28	57.834	97.0
Span (ft)	46.800	23.069	62.08
Average chord aft of hinge line (ft) .	1.90	2.50	1.58
Chord (% of control surface chord) . .	20	20	25
Tab travel (degrees)	9° down 15° up	15° L & R	15° down 15° up

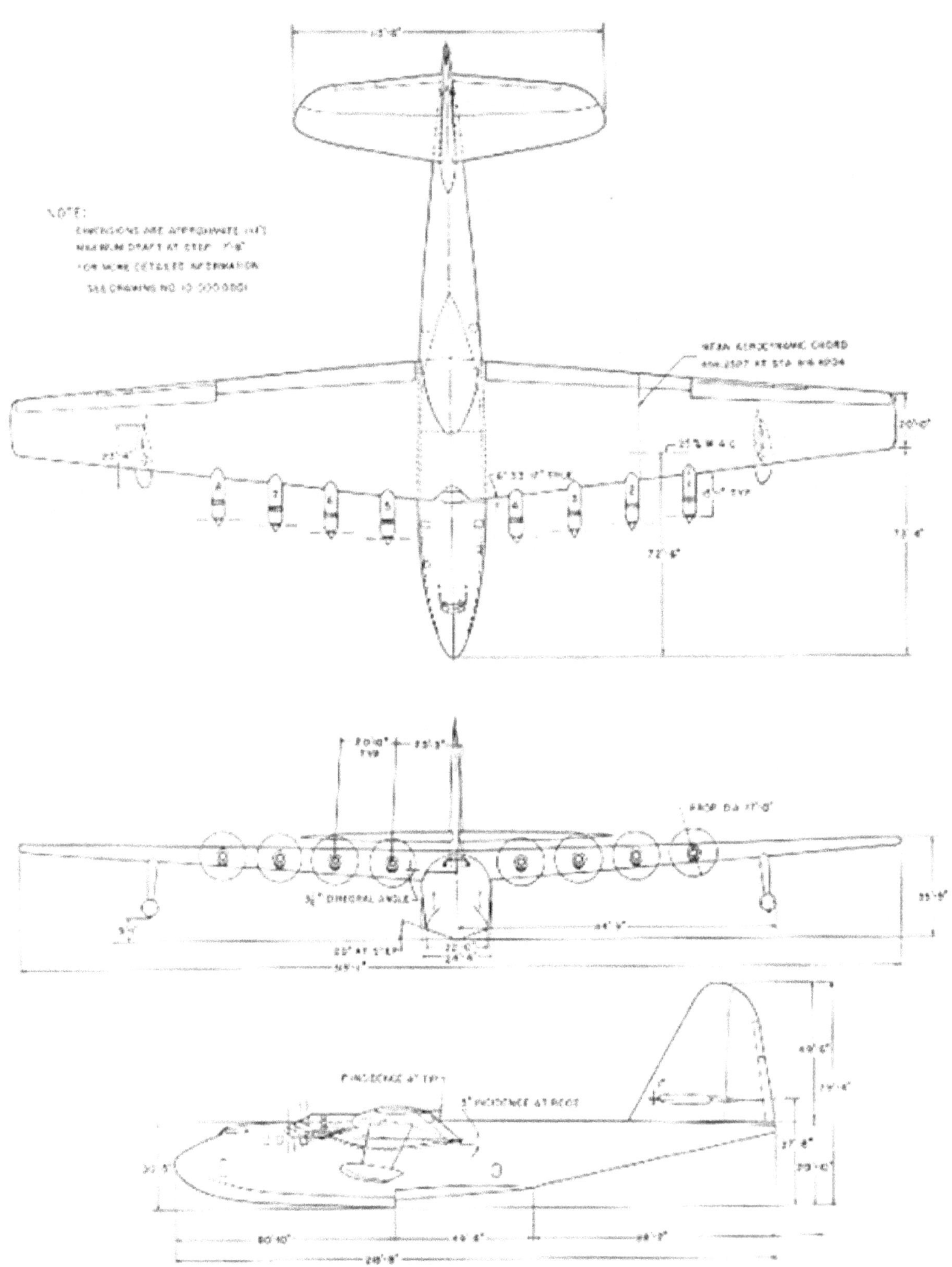

(d) Trim Tabs -

	Elevator Trim Tabs	Rudder Trim Tabs	Aileron Trim Tabs
Area aft of hinge line (sq ft) . .	48.38	22.503	33.6
Span (ft)	15.526	11.875	25.0
Mean geometric chord (ft)	1.58	1.90	1.35
Chord (% of control surface chord) . .	20	20	25
Tab travel (degrees)	15° up 15° down	15° up 15° down	15° up 15° down

1-1.3 Performance -

	Gross Weight 350,000 lb	Gross Weight 400,000 lb
High speed at sea level with T. O. power (mph)	235.5	234
High speed at sea level with normal rated power (mph)	222	218
High speed at 5000 ft with normal rated power (mph)	231	227
Operating speed at sea level with max. cruising power, 1675 BHP/2230 rpm (mph)	190	185
Initial cruising speed for max. range at 5000 ft altitude (mph) . .	141	150
Landing speed at sea level - 10% above stall, 45° flap (mph)	81	87
Range in miles at best cruising speed with no fuel reserve (8 engines)		
12,500 gal. fuel . .	---	2,975
6,000 gal. fuel . .	1,575	1,430
Endurance in hours at best cruising speed (8 engines)		
12,500 gal. fuel . .	---	20.9
6,000 gal. fuel . .	11.5	9.5

	Gross Weight 350,000 lb	Gross Weight 400,000 lb
Service ceiling (ft)	20,900	17,400
Rate of climb at sea level with normal rated power (ft/min)	878	675
Rate of climb at sea level with T.O. power (ft/min)	1,134	916
Time to climb to 5000 ft altitude with normal rated power (min) . . .	5.9	7.7

1-1.4 Hull - The hull interior is divided structurally into an upper (flight) and a lower (cargo) deck with the bilge below the cargo deck.

(a) Cargo Deck - The cargo deck is arranged as follows:

1. The forward cargo deck section contains the overhead removable section of the nose, mooring and anchoring facilities, auxiliary hydraulic pumps, and the port and starboard access doors.

2. The middle cargo deck section includes 15,640 cubic feet of stowage space, portable hand operated bilge pumps, fixed electric bilge pumps and equipment, auxiliary hydraulic station, two air compressors, a stowage cabinet, ventilating equipment, portable service ladders, CO_2 bottles, and aft port and starboard access doors. The circular stairway leading to the flight deck is located in this section on the forward starboard side.

3. The aft cargo deck section includes the catwalk leading to the tail section, the empennage inspection doors, and the permanently installed rudder service ladder.

(b) Bilge - Below the cargo deck the bilge includes two permanent water ballast tanks, watertight compartments and inspection doors, fuel pumps, 8 fuel storage tanks and fuel compartment ventilating system.

(c) Flight Deck - On the flight deck, which is located above the cargo deck and forward of the wing, are the pilot's and copilot's stations mounted on a dais at the forward end of the deck, the flight engineer's station located directly aft of the copilot, and the radio operator's station located aft of the pilot. Aft of the flight crew stations are the off duty seats for the crew, flight test equipment, auxiliary power units, battery junction box, oil reservoir, stowage cabinet, emergency equipment, thermos bottles, wing access doors, and overhead hatch.

1-1.5 Wing - The wing consists of port and starboard wing panels, wing fairing, wing tips, eight nacelles, flaps, ailerons, and aileron trim and flying tabs. An interior wing walkway affords access to all engine nacelles, wing tanks, plumbing, and electrical equipment.

1-1.6 Wing Floats - The two fixed type floats are attached to the underside of each wing at station 1329. They are divided into 5 watertight bulkheads, each being provided with an inspection hatch. Grip rings for mooring are installed on the outboard side of each float. Access to the interior is through an entrance hatch located on the topside of the float at float station 56.

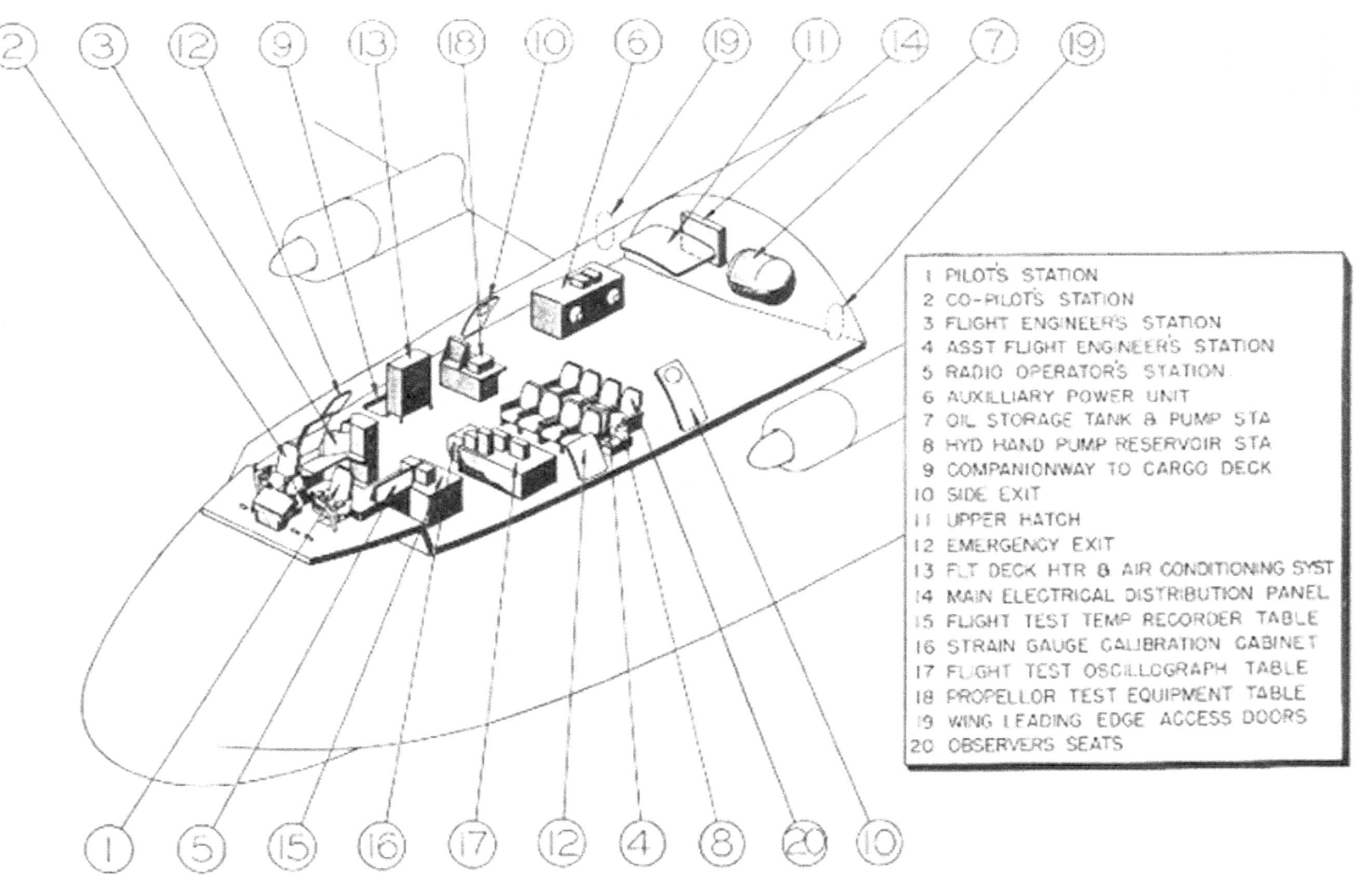

FLIGHT DECK ARRANGEMENT

1-2 ENGINES -

1-2.1 General - The airplane is powered by eight Pratt and Whitney R-4360-4A engines, conventionally mounted in the leading edges of port and starboard wings.

(a) Specifications -

Type	-	28 cylinder, four-row air cooled, radial
Bore	-	5.75 in.
Stroke	-	6.00 in.
Displacement	-	4360 cu in.
Compression Ratio	-	7:1
Supercharger	-	Single Stage
Impeller Ratio	-	6.08:1 (fixed low ratio hyd couplings)
Propeller Reduction Gear Ratio	-	0.425:1
Magnetos	-	Scintilla D4RN-2
Carburetor	-	Stromberg PR-100 B3
Fuel	-	MIL-F-5572, Grade 100/130 2cc/gal. max. TEL
Oil	-	MIL-L-6082, Grade 1100

(b) Engine Ratings -

	BHP	RPM	Critical Altitude
Takeoff (5 min max.)	3000	2700	1700
Normal rated	2500	2550	5000
Max. auto lean	1675	2230	10750
Max. overspeed (30 sec)		3060	
Max. bmep 202			

(c) Cylinder Arrangement - Each of the seven banks of four cylinders is arranged helically about the crankcase. Deflector baffles direct the cooling air stream the entire length of each bank and individual baffles guide the air over the finned surfaces of each cylinder.

(d) Reduction Gear and Torquemeter - The propeller reduction gearing and torquemeter are incorporated in the magneto drive case of the engine. The propeller reduction gear ratio is 0.425:1. Engine torquemeter indicators are located on the flight engineer's engine panel and the pilot's engine instrument panel.

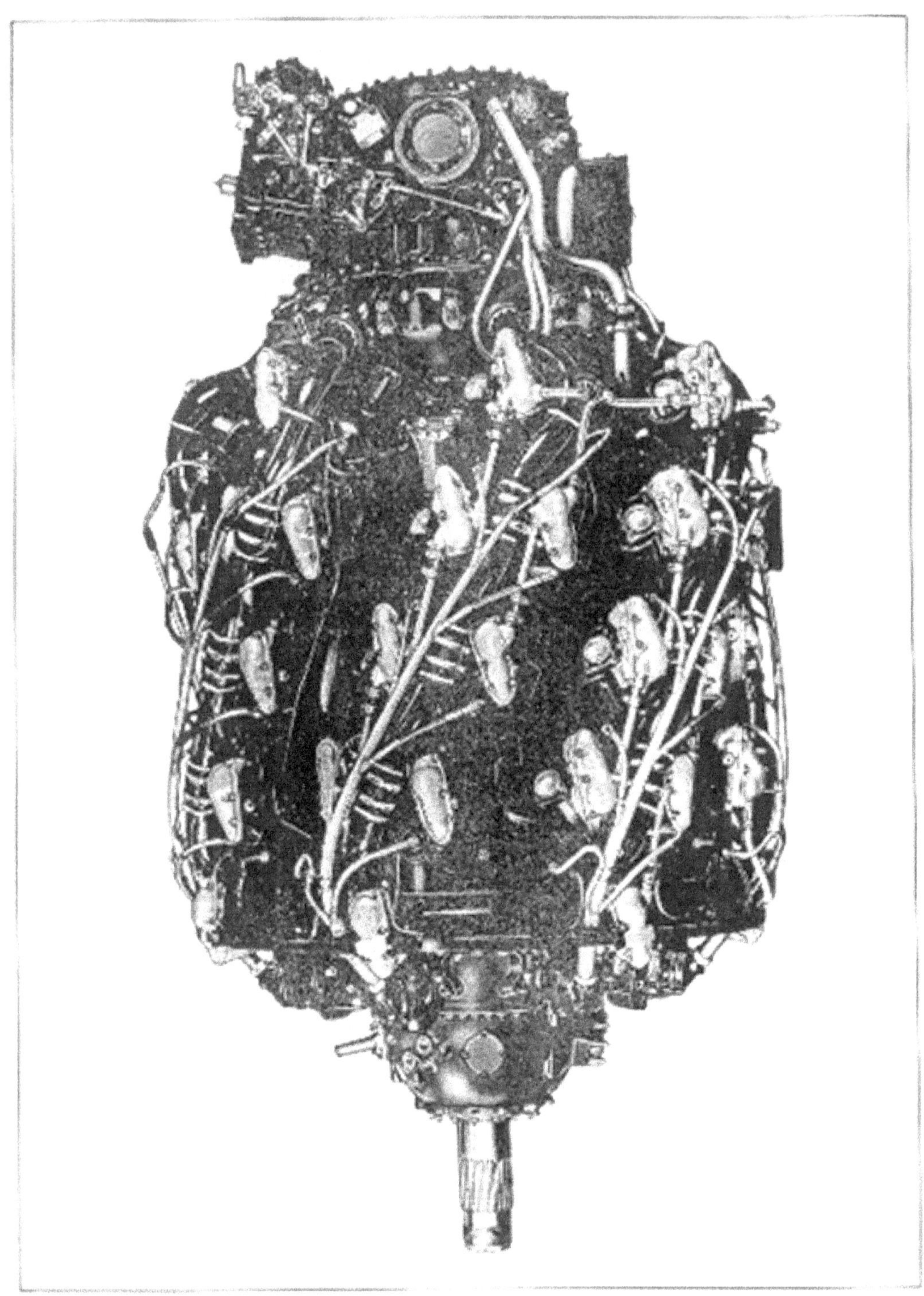

R-4360-4A ENGINE

1-2. 2 Throttles - An electrical servo throttle control system operates from the 115V DC electrical system and consists of an electrical potentiometer mechanically connected to each throttle lever. The electrical potentiometers are wired to servo units located in each nacelle and the servo units are mechanically connected to the carburetors. Full travel of throttle operation from full open to full close can be obtained in approximately one second. When the throttle lever moves the electrical potentiometer, the servo unit positions the throttle valves in the carburetors which respond to throttle lever motion in .03 seconds. A throttle inching control system operates through an independent system which primarily consists of a separate motor mounted on each servo unit and controlled from either the pilot's or flight engineer's station by toggle switches. There is a mechanical override provided in each nacelle in case both the primary throttle control and throttle inching systems fail. For further details, refer to Chapter 7-1.

1-2. 3 Carburetion - The engines are equipped with Bendix Stromberg PR-100 B3 pressure type carburetors. The carburetor mixture control levers are located on the flight engineer's engine panel. Heater air can be furnished to the carburetor by opening an alternate air valve which admits engine heated air into the carburetor intake duct. This valve is controlled by an electric actuator operated by a switch on the flight engineer's engine panel.

1-2. 4 Engine Cooling - The amount of cooling air passing over the engine is regulated by cowl flap position which is controlled by a switch on the flight engineer's engine panel. For cooling the engine oil, two 16" diameter oil coolers are installed in parallel air ducts on the under side of each nacelle. Oil cooler airflow is controlled by means of an exit flap, the position of which is determined automatically by the temperature of the engine oil. There is a manual override control for the oil cooler flap which can be operated from the flight engineer's engine panel. For further details, refer to Chapter 7-3.

1-2. 5 Ignition System - Seven dual magnetos furnish ignition for each engine and are mounted forward of the front row of cylinders on the magneto drive case. Ground switches for the magnetos are located on the flight engineer's engine panel. For further details, refer to Chapter 7-1.

1-2. 6 Starting System - Starting is accomplished by means of direct drive starters, powered by the auxiliary power unit (APU) located on the flight deck, or from an outside source through the external power receptacles. High tension voltage for starting is furnished by an ignition booster coil. An electrically operated solenoid valve is connected to the carburetor fuel inlet line for the purpose of supplying fuel directly into the blower case to facilitate starting of the engines. The primer control switches are located on the flight engineer's engine panel.

FLIGHT ENGINEER'S ENGINE PANEL

OIL SYSTEM CONTROL PANEL

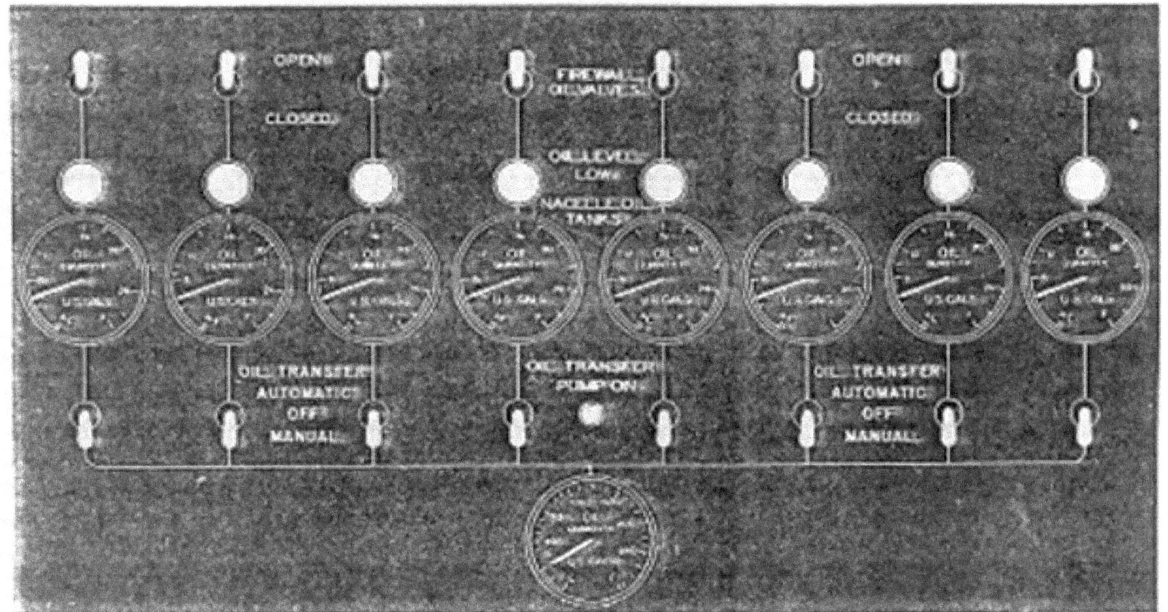

OIL TRANSFER SYSTEM SCHEMATIC

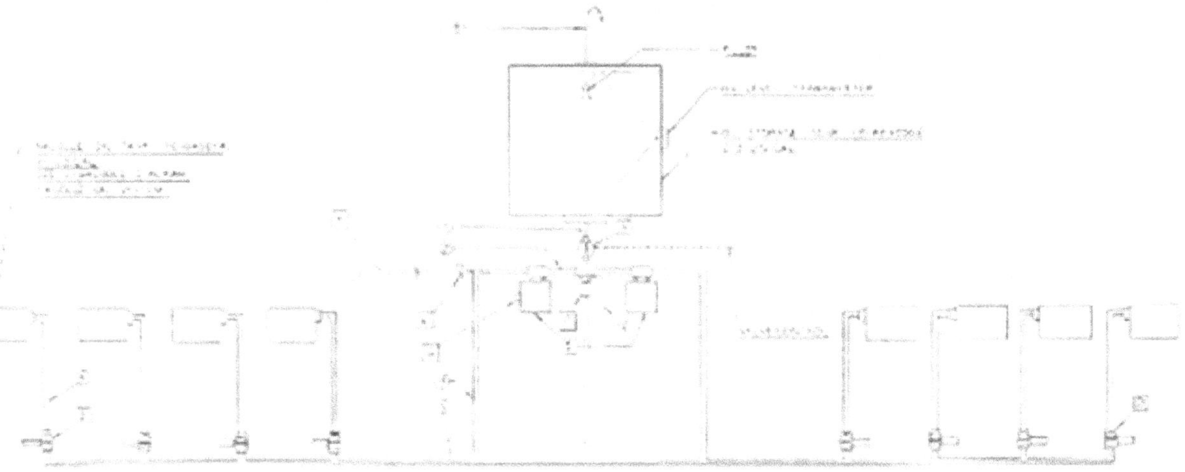

1-3 PROPELLERS -

1-3.1 General - The airplane is equipped with eight Hamilton Standard, single rotation, four blade full feathering non-reversible propellers with Hub No. 24F60-35. For taxi tests, seven of the propellers are Blade No. 6497A-0, 17'2" diameter and the eighth located on Engine 4, is Blade No. 6521A-12, 16'2" diameter. An electric driven pump supplies oil pressure for feathering and unfeathering.

1-3.2 Governor Control - An electrically controlled double acting governor controls the pitch changing mechanism in the propeller hub. During synchronized operation, governor control is obtained by movement of the prop synchronizer lever, located on the pilot's control pedestal. The same control is obtained through a momentary switch located directly below the prop synchronizer lever. A synchronizer override propeller control switch is located adjacent to the momentary switch on the pilot's control panel. Individual propeller control switches are provided on the flight engineer's engine panel. For further details refer to Chapter 7-2.

1-3.3 Synchronizer Control - The propeller pitch and engine rpm are controlled by 3 type C4 Hamilton Standard Propeller Synchronizers, mechanically linked to operate simultaneously. Constant synchronous speed of all 8 engines is maintained with a minimum of control. The pilot controls the engine rpm by means of the Propeller Synchronizer Lever located just to the right of the pilot's throttles on the control pedestal quandrant. The master engine (No. 2 or No. 3) is selected by a control switch on the pilot's pedestal directly below the Prop Synchronizer Lever. Manual control of prop pitch is by means of the Mom (momentary) switch to the right of the master engine selector switch. To the right of the momentary switch is a Fixed Prop RPM control switch which is a synchronizer override switch and will cause the propellers to go to the maximum or minimum rpm position. The flight engineer's station is equipped with individual momentary toggle switches for each engine to affect minor changes in engine rpm or to control the pitch manually.

1-4 OIL SYSTEM -

1-4.1 General - The oil system provides lubricating oil for the eight engines and oil for propeller feathering. Engine oil tanks of 31 gallon capacity are located in each engine nacelle, and a reserve tank of 281 gallon capacity is located on the flight deck mounted on the forward face of the front spar. A transfer pump system controlled automatically or manually by switches located on the flight engineer's oil system panel, replenishes oil in the nacelle tanks. When this system is on AUTOMATIC, a float inside each nacelle tank actuates the transfer pump circuit which maintains the oil at the proper operating level. For further details refer to Chapter 7-3.

1-4.2 Indicator Lights -

(a) Low level warning lights located on the oil system control panel become illuminated when the oil level in the nacelle oil tanks drops below 15 gallons.

(b) Low oil pressure warning lights located on flight engineer's engine panel become illuminated when the oil pressure drops to 50 psi.

1-4.3 Oil Dilution - This airplane is not provided with an oil dilution system and the Oil Dil (dilution) switches located across the top of flight engineer's engine panel are inoperative.

NACELLE OIL SYSTEM SCHEMATIC

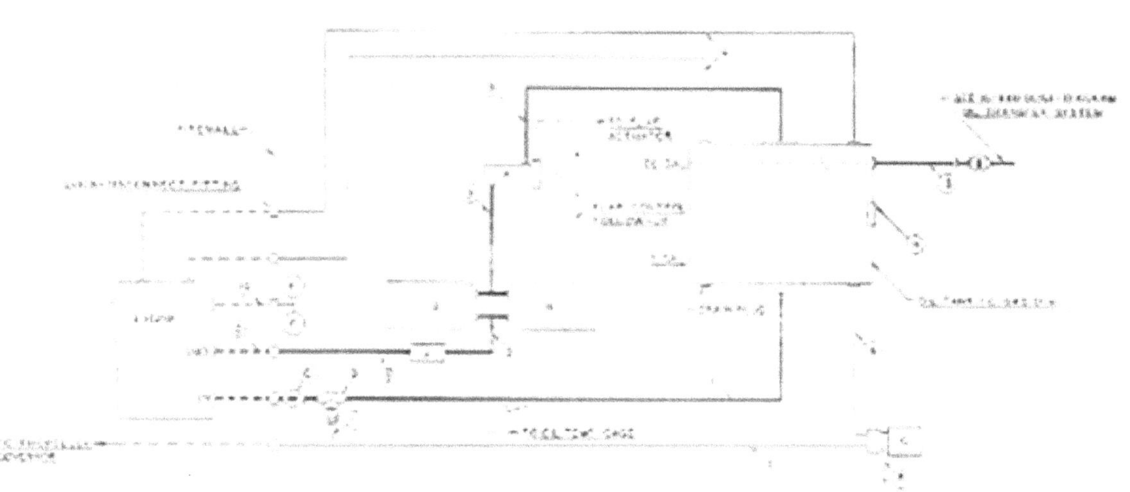

1-5 FUEL SYSTEM -

1-5.1 General - The fuel system is a single-point loading system with fuel storage provided by hull fuel tanks and wing operating tanks. In addition to the regular system for delivering fuel from the tanks to the engines, there is available an entirely separate emergency fuel system.

1-5.2 Fuel Tanks - The main fuel tanks are located in the bilge of the hull. There are eight hull tanks installed at present, with provision for installation of fourteen. Two of these eight, tanks 5 and 6, are standbys, being connected to the regular fuel system, but to be used only in an emergency, as in the case of a leak in one of the filled tanks. By proper use of the shutoff valves, part of the fuel can be transferred by gravity from one tank to another. The normal fuel capacity of each hull tank is 900 U.S. gallons with fuel quantities being indicated on the flight engineer's fuel system panel. Two wing tanks with a normal capacity of 300 U.S. gallons are provided, one tank in the leading edge of each wing inboard of engines No. 4 and No. 5. Hull tank No. 8 contains reserve fuel and under all operating conditions should be used last as it is connected directly to the emergency fuel system.

1-5.3 Fuel Route - Normally fuel is supplied from the hull tanks to the wing tanks, which in turn, supply fuel directly to the engines. Under normal system operation, each transfer pump delivers the fuel from the hull tank manifold to its wing tank. Each wing tank then supplies fuel through a manifold to four engines, two on each wing. The two manifolds have a manually operated crossfeed located on the front spar which is normally closed. The rate of fuel flow is measured at each engine and is remotely indicated on the flight engineer's engine panel. Under emergency conditions however, the emergency fuel system delivers fuel directly from the hull tanks to the engines. Either or both of two emergency transfer pumps can draw fuel from the hull tank supply manifold, or directly from Tank No. 8, should the manifold system become inoperative.

1-5.4 Fuel Booster Pumps - Electrically driven booster pumps are provided in the engine fuel supply manifolds between the wing tanks and the engines. Two booster pumps are located in each manifold, each pump supplying two engines. For cruise fuel requirements the booster pumps are off and the fuel flows from the wing tanks through the booster pump by-pass, to the engine driven fuel pump located on each engine. The booster pumps are operated by switches located on the flight engineer's fuel panel. The booster pumps and engine driven fuel pumps are equipped with by-pass reliefs, set to maintain 25 ± 1 psi carburetor pressure. Fuel system pressures, measured at the carburetor, are indicated on the flight engineer's engine panel.

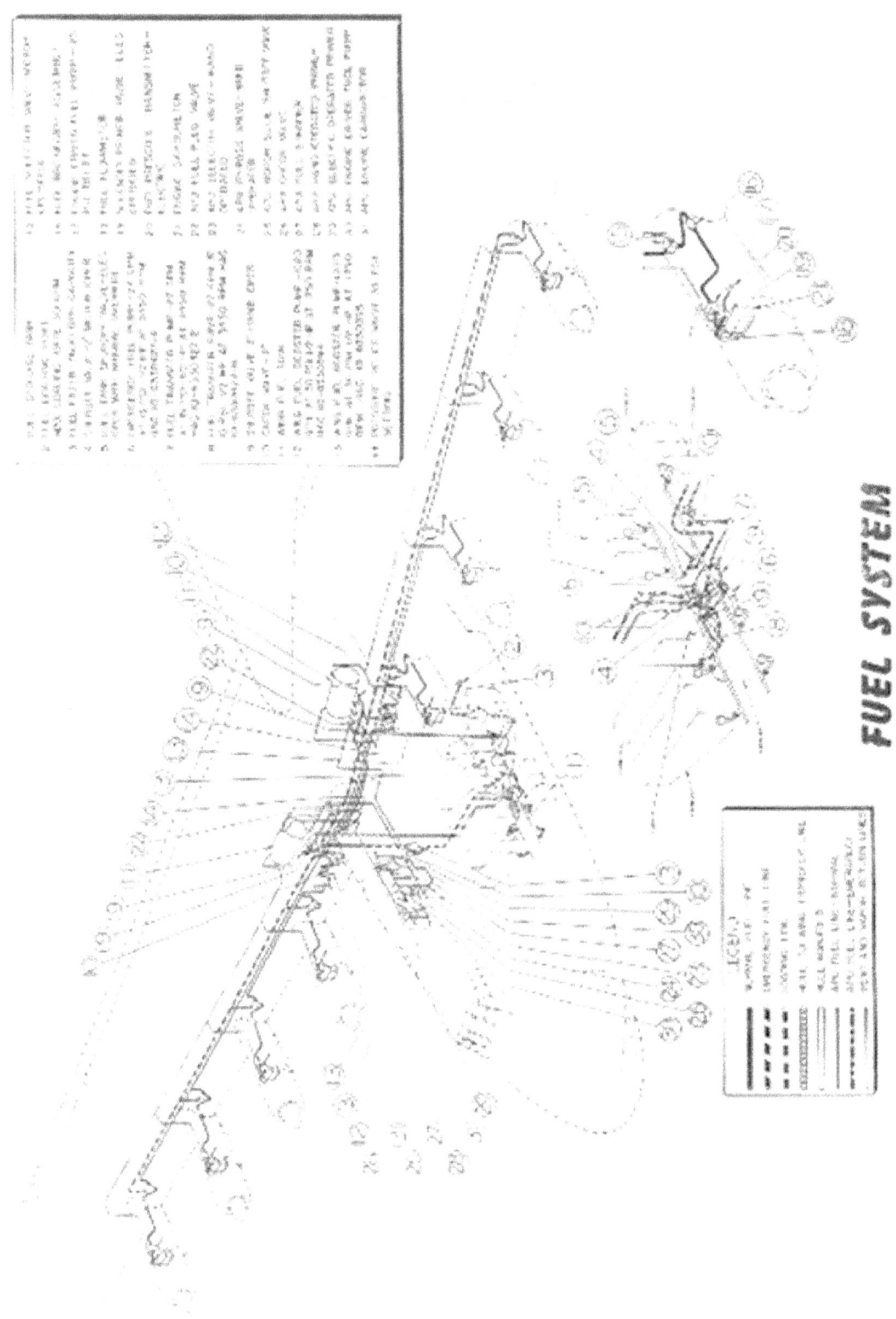
FUEL SYSTEM

FUEL SYSTEM - SCHEMATIC

Dwg No. 10-6300124

UNIT	MFG NO.
HULL STORAGE TANK	[illegible]
[illegible]	[illegible] - HULL TANKS
	[illegible] - WING TANKS
FAN (ELEC)	[illegible]
	[illegible] AIR MOTOR [illegible]
FUEL TANK WATER DRAIN VALVE (MANUAL)	[illegible]
FUEL TANK SHUTOFF VALVE (ELEC) WITH MANUAL OVERRIDE	[illegible] MANUAL OVERRIDE [illegible] WHITTAKER VALVE [illegible]
WING FUEL TANK	[illegible]
CHECK VALVE [illegible]	[illegible]
FUEL TRANSFER PUMP [illegible]	[illegible]
SHUTOFF VALVE [illegible] (ELEC)	[illegible] MANUAL OVERRIDE [illegible] VALVE
EMERGENCY FUEL PUMP [illegible]	[illegible]
[illegible] DRAIN VALVE	[illegible]
FUEL FILTER [illegible]	[illegible]
PUMP SEAL DRAIN TANK	[illegible]

ITEM	UNIT	MFG NO.
[illegible]	FUEL TANK WATER DRAIN NOZZLE	[illegible]
[illegible]	SHUTOFF VALVE [illegible] (MANUAL)	WHITTAKER [illegible]
[illegible]	PRESSURE RELIEF VALVE [illegible]	PARKER [illegible]
17	FUEL SELECTOR VALVE (ELEC)	PARKER [illegible] VALVE [illegible] MOTOR
18	WING FUEL BOOSTER PUMP [illegible]	PESCO [illegible] AAF TYPE [illegible] MOTOR [illegible]
[illegible]	APU SELECTOR VALVE (MANUAL)	WHITTAKER [illegible]
[illegible]	APU [illegible] VALVE (MANUAL)	[illegible]
[illegible]	APU [illegible] RELIEF VALVE	WHITTAKER [illegible]
[illegible]	APU CHECK VALVE	WHITTAKER [illegible]
[illegible]	APU FUEL STRAINER	[illegible]
[illegible]	APU PRIMER (MANUAL)	[illegible]
[illegible]	APU PRIMER (ELEC)	[illegible]
[illegible]	APU ENGINE DRIVEN FUEL PUMP	[illegible]
[illegible]	FUEL PRESSURE TRANSMITTER (ELEC)	[illegible]
[illegible]	[illegible] PRIMER VALVE (ELEC)	[illegible]
[illegible]	ENGINE DRIVEN PUMP [illegible] RELIEF	[illegible]
[illegible]	FUEL FLOWMETER	[illegible]
[illegible]	[illegible] SHUTOFF VALVE (MANUAL)	WHITTAKER [illegible]
[illegible]	APU FUEL [illegible] VALVE	WHITTAKER [illegible]
[illegible]	FUEL PUMP SEAL DRAIN PUMP	[illegible] PUMP [illegible] MOTOR

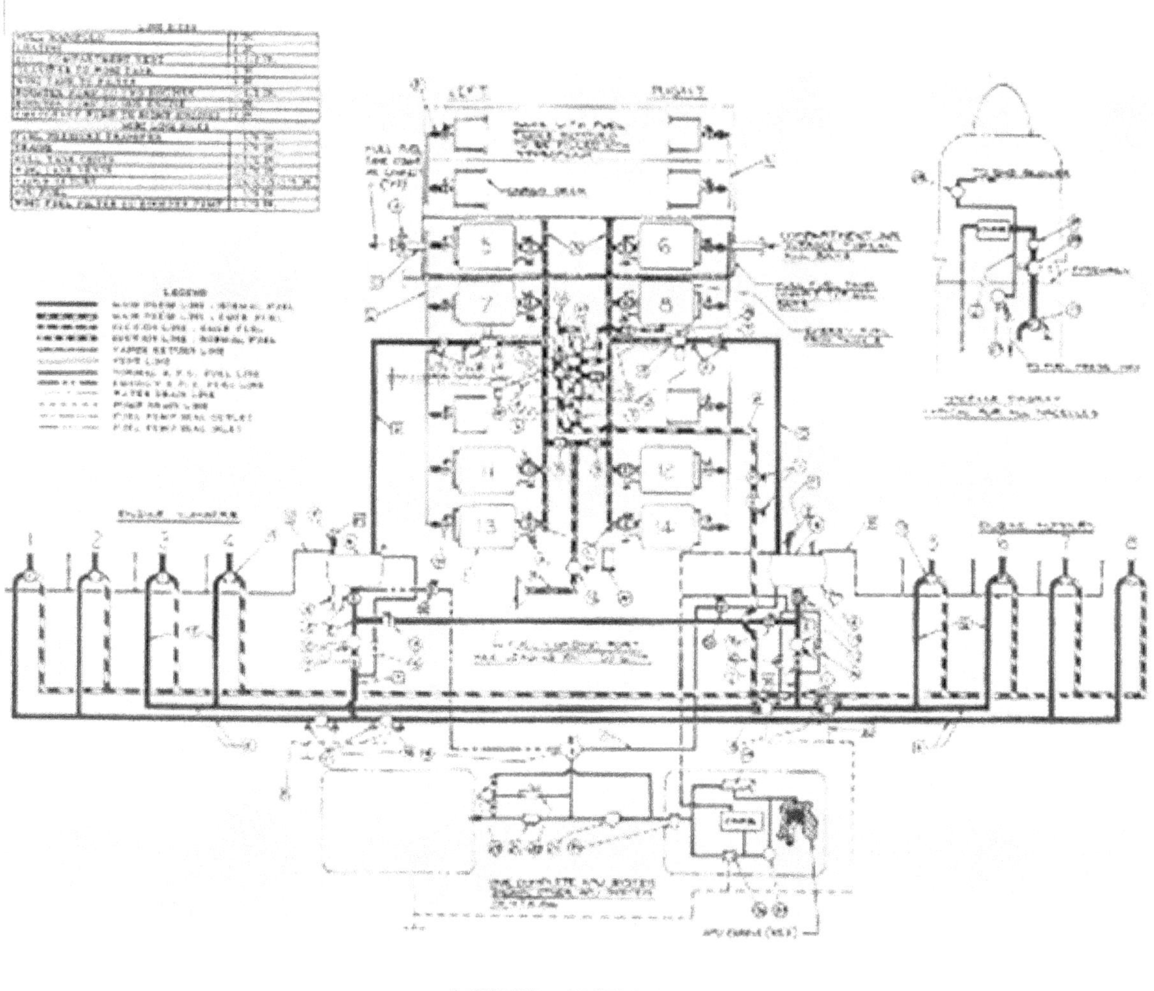

FUEL SYSTEM CONTROL PANELS

1-5.5 Emergency Fuel System - In case of emergency, two electrically driven centrifugal type emergency fuel pumps installed in the hull fuel compartment can transfer fuel from any hull tank directly to the engine firewall fuel shutoff and selector valve. At the firewall fuel shutoff valve the fuel rejoins the normal fuel system leading to the carburetors. In addition to containing the reserve fuel, No. 8 hull tank is the designated emergency tank and is provided with an extra valved outlet (in addition to the regular system manifold outlet) which feeds directly to the emergency pumping system. No. 8 tank should always be filled to its normal 900 gallon capacity before takeoff.

1-5.6 Hull Tank Compartment Vent System - Each hull tank compartment is provided with an individual ventilating system. Fresh air is drawn in on the starboard side of the airplane through ducts that lead down into the fuel tank compartments under the main cargo deck where it is permitted to circulate freely. It is then exhausted through ducts on the port side of the airplane by electrically operated blowers located at the outlet.

1-5.7 Fuel for Auxiliary Power Units - Normal fuel supply for operation of the auxiliary power units is from the right wing fuel tank. Emergency fuel supply for the APUs is from the left wing tank. A manually operated selector valve, located in a recess in the lower front panel of the APU cabinet, is provided for selection of normal or emergency fuel supply system.

1-5.8 Indicator Lights - Fuel pressure warnings, fuel quantity warnings, and various other critical fuel system operating information are indicated by a series of indicator lights located on the flight engineer's panels. The various limiting values indicated by the lights are listed in Chapter 7-4.

1-6 ELECTRICAL SYSTEM -

1-6.1 General - Direct and alternating current are provided for the operation of electrical equipment. DC power is supplied by three main engine driven generators, or by batteries. Seven inverters operate on DC power and furnish current for units operating on alternating current. Two 120V DC auxiliary power units are provided to supply power, under restrictions. Power from an outside source can be supplied through external receptacles when the airplane is in the dock or anchored in the harbor.

1-6.2 DC Power Supply -

(a) Generators - A 15 KW, 120V DC generator is mounted on the accessory drive section of engines 1, 3, and 7. These three generators provide 120V DC power for the airplane under all normal operating conditions. There are also two 30 KW, 120V DC auxiliary power units (APUs), which are located on the right side of the flight deck just forward of the wing leading edge access door. The APUs are driven by four-cylinder air cooled engines and their use is restricted to an emergency, such as failure of engine driven generators, or in case the electrical loads exceed engine driven generator capacity (see Chapter 4-7).

(b) Batteries - The main storage battery power system consists of two separate banks of nine, series-connected, 12V storage batteries, each bank providing 104V DC. The batteries are contained in vented boxes located on the forward cargo deck. There is also provided a 24V battery system for starting the APUs and supplying current to the hull entrance lights, anchor lights, etc. The 24V system is composed of two 12V batteries connected in series and located on the flight deck just forward of the APU cabinets.

(c) Dynamotors - Two dynamotors of 90 ampere rating are provided to furnish 24V DC output for operation of the 24V circuits and for charging the 24V batteries. Either dynamotor may be operated independently, or both may be operated in parallel if the load warrants parallel operation. A separate 24V DC dynamotor is also provided to furnish current necessary for operation of the combustible gas alarm. All three dynamotors receive their input current from the main power 120V DC system.

(d) External Power Supply - Separate receptacles are provided for connecting external power sources to the airplane during standby operations. For detailed information see Chapter 7-5.

1-6.3 DC Instruments and Equipment - Several of the instruments and indicating circuits are operated directly from the main 120V DC power supply utilizing suitable dropping resistors. See Chapter 7-5 for further details.

ELECTRICAL INSTRUMENT PANEL

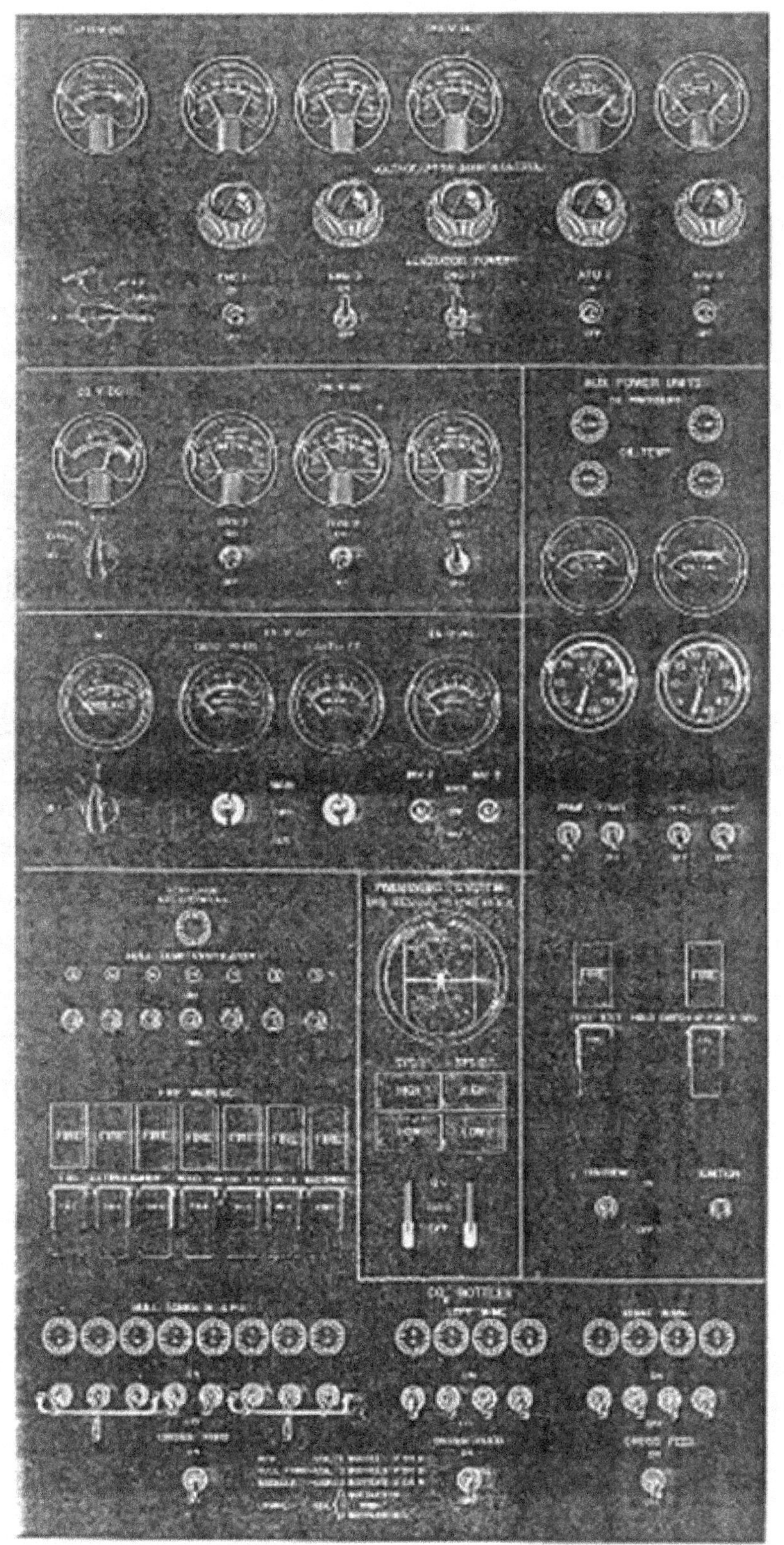

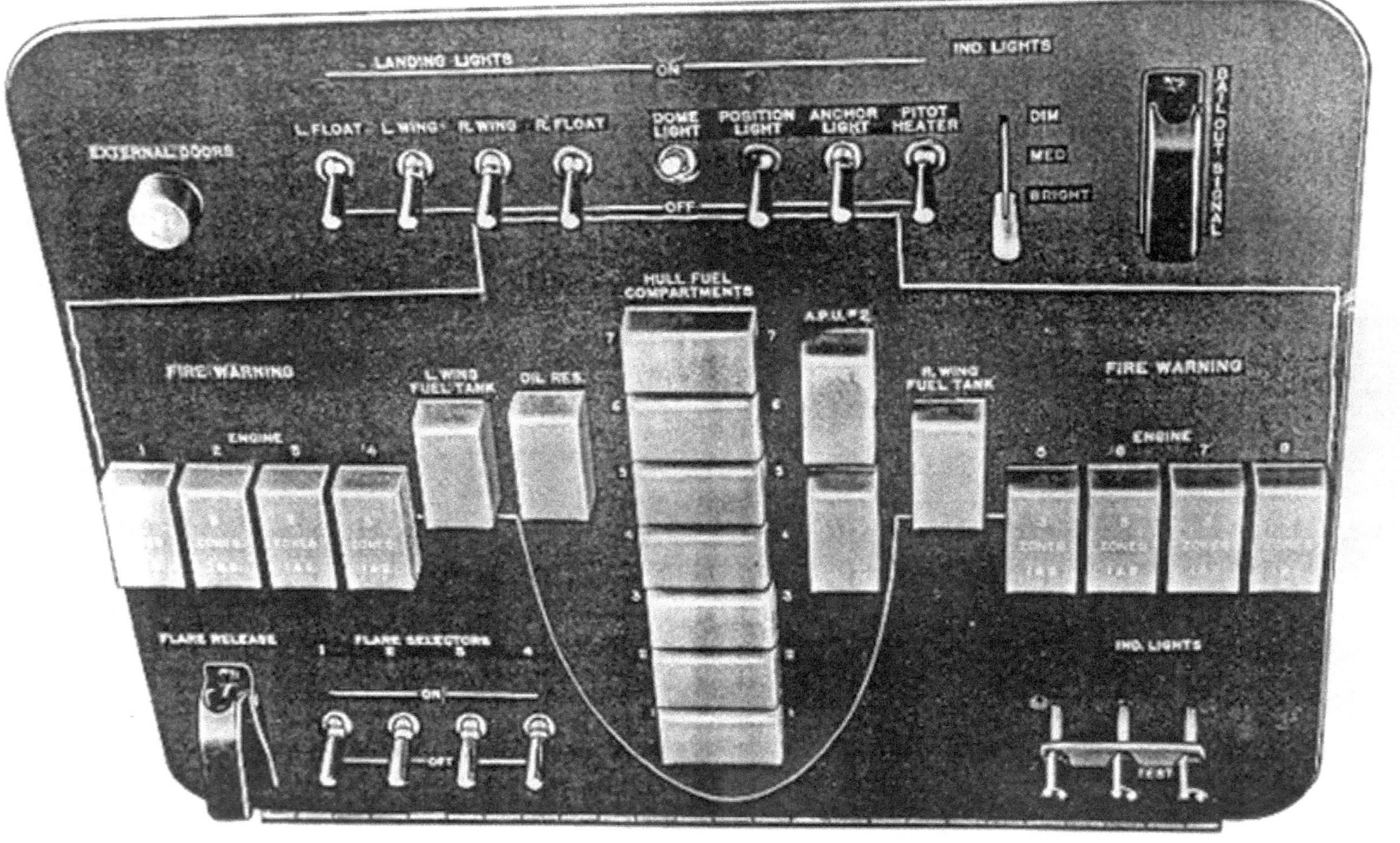

PILOT'S OVERHEAD INSTRUMENT PANEL

FUEL AND FLOAT COMPARTMENT
BLOWER CONTROL PANEL

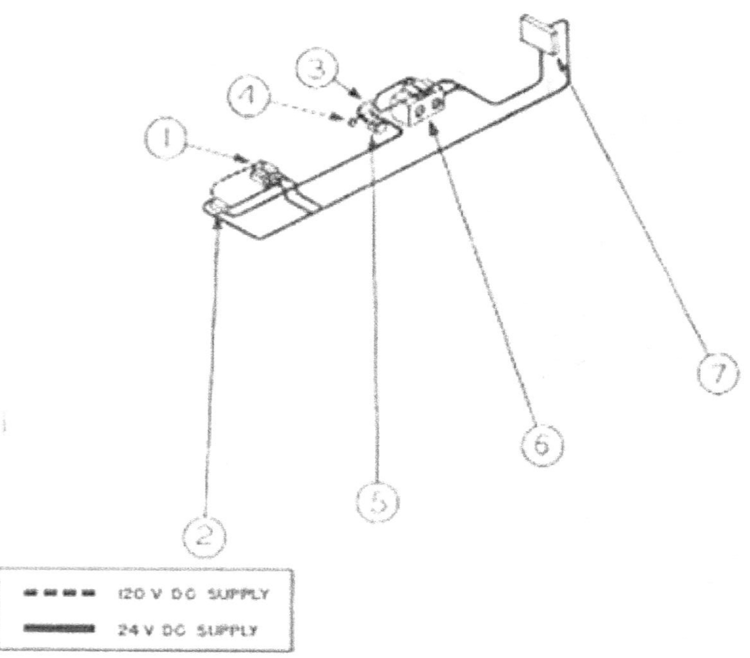

LEGEND

1 DYNAMOTOR (POWERED BY 120 V DC)
2 FLT ENGR JCT BOX
3 BATTERY RELAY JCT BOX
4 24 V DC EXT POWER RECP
5 24 V DC BATTERY SUPPLY
6 24V DC APU SUPPLY
7 NEG BUS MAIN JCT BOX

24 VOLT DC POWER SUPPLY CIRCUIT

1-6.4 AC Power Supply - Seven inverters are provided to furnish current for units operating on alternate current. All seven receive their input current from the main 120V DC system.

1-6.5 AC Instruments and Equipment - A 26V, 3 phase (400 cycle) AC instrumentation system is employed and is energized from two of the seven inverters (see Paragraph 1-6.4) which receive their input current from the main 120V DC system. The two inverters cannot be operated simultaneously and selection should be alternated to equalize wear on both inverters. Inverter input power may be changed to battery power through switches located on flight engineer's electrical instrument panel and switches located on auxiliary hydraulic panel.

1-6.6 Flight Control Circuits - Power sources for the auto pilot and auto flying tab inverters (see Chapter 7-5) are selected by the flight engineer from the main 120V DC system or the auxiliary battery system in emergency. Selection of large or small inverter is accomplished by a switch located on the pilot's pedestal and a switch on the auxiliary hydraulic control panel. Power is supplied to the auto pilot through a power switch located on the pilot's pedestal. Switches controlling aileron, rudder, and elevator trim tabs are located at the pilot's and copilot's side of the pilots' pedestal. The master trim tab control is at the pilot's station. A master changeover switch located on the pilot's pedestal energizes electrical circuits to the hydraulic control, artificial feel, FT control, and FT switches.

1-6.7 Auxiliary Power Unit - Two Jack and Heintz 30 KW, 120V DC auxiliary power units are located on the starboard side of the flight deck just forward of the wing leading edge access door. The electrical generators of the units supply power to the 120V DC system and are operated by two Franklin air-cooled, four cylinder gasoline engines developing 113 hp each. The operating switches, ammeters, cylinder head temperature gauges, tachometers, and oil pressure and temperature warning lights are located on the flight engineer's electrical instrument panel. Two control boxes are mounted on top of the APU cabinet and a manual voltage ,control and rheostat panel is located directly above these two boxes.

1-7 FLIGHT CONTROL SYSTEMS - Dual column and wheel, elevator and aileron controls are provided, as well as pedal type rudder controls, for both pilot and co-pilot. Ordinarily operation of the flight control system is accomplished by the hydraulic system; however, a separate flying tab system is provided as an alternate or emergency flight control system. Normal control of this system is through the control column and pedals, or it may be operated through the electrically actuated auto flying tab system. In addition, there is also provided an electrically operated trim tab system.

1-7.1 Hydraulic System - The hydraulic system is a 2000 psi system and includes a main power system, auxiliary power system, and hand pump system. It is a direct power system mechanically connected to the control surfaces and capable of supplying all the power required for their actuation. Under normal conditions, the main power system supplies power for operating the ailerons, rudder, elevators, and wing flaps; however, in an emergency, hydraulic power is supplied by the auxiliary system. The ailerons, rudder, and elevators employ dual systems completely independent of each other, in which all functional units (cylinders, valves, etc.) necessary for operation are duplicated. The flap system employs only one group of operational units, but either No. 1 or No. 2 main system pressure may be selected to provide the power required. Power is supplied to each system (No. 1 and No. 2) by either the engine driven pumps or the auxiliary electric motor driven pumps, but not from both simultaneously. It is possible to fly with one system connected to one surface, the other system on another surface, and both systems on a third surface. The auxiliary pumps do not supply power to the flaps.

(a) Main System - The main hydraulic power source is composed of two identical independent systems referred to as No. 1 and No. 2 main systems, each system being powered by two engine driven pumps. The pumps for No. 1 main system are mounted on the accessory drive section of engines 2 and 4. Pumps for No. 2 main system are similarly mounted on engines 5 and 6. Under normal operating conditions both main systems are used simultaneously, each supplying one half the total power requirements; however, either system is capable of supplying total power demands and will do so automatically in the event of loss of the other system.

(b) Auxiliary Power System - This system is composed of two identical, independent systems referred to as No. 1 and No. 2, each system being powered by one electrically driven pump. These are emergency systems and since their power source is from storage batteries, their output time is limited. This system uses the same surface control units as the main systems; however, there is no interflow between systems.

(c) Hand Pump System - This system is completely independent of either the main or auxiliary systems. It is a service system which provides power to operate by-pass valves, changeover overrides, and gust locks, and is composed of two units referred to as the regular system which is capable of operating all units of the service group, and the alternate system which can be used only to operate the by-pass valves. Initial pressure can be supplied by No. 1 main system prior

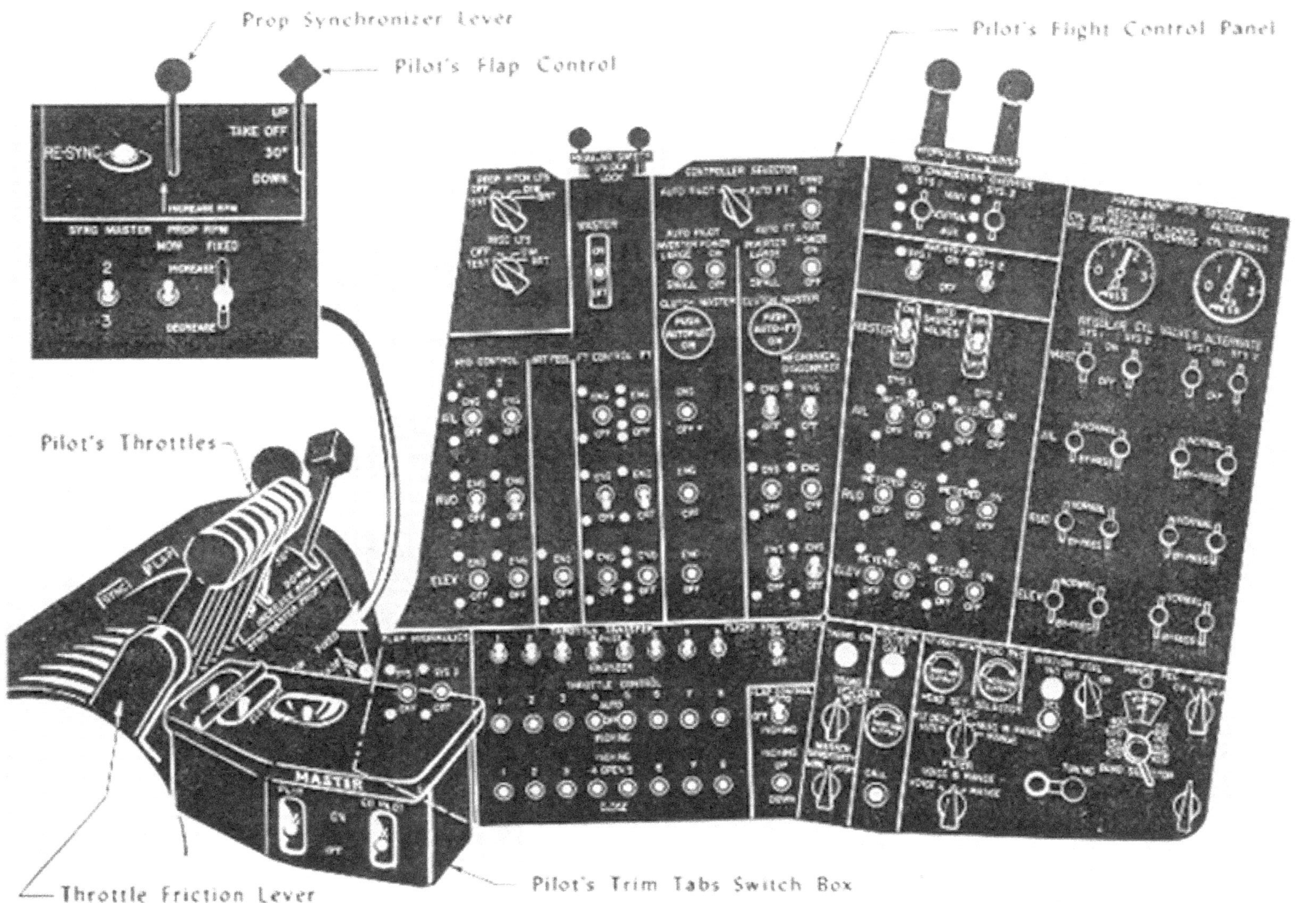

PILOT'S CONTROL PEDESTAL

to takeoff. All subsequent requirements are supplied by a hand pump located at the co-pilot's station.

1-7.2 Flying Tab System - This system is separate from the hydraulic flight control system and affords a means of emergency control of the airplane in event of complete hydraulic system failure. It is normally operated manually through the control column and pedals or through the auto flying tab system. Controls to the left of the pilot's seat actuate auto pilot servos connected to the flying tabs. There are two elevator tabs, two aileron tabs, and one rudder tab.

1-7.3 Changeover Controls - The controls to change from hydraulic system operation to flying tab operation and vice versa are located on the pilot's pedestal. Detailed procedure is outlined in Chapter 7-6.

1-7.4 Trim Tab System - Electrically actuated trim tabs are provided for all primary flight control surfaces. They are completely separate and independent from the primary flight control systems and are actuated by toggle switches located on the pilot's and co-pilot's control pedestals. There are two elevator, one rudder, and two aileron trim tabs. Additional descriptive information will be found in Chapter 7-6.

1-7.5 Flaps - Single slotted type flaps are located on the inboard trailing edge of each wing, and are controlled hydraulically by means of two levers adjacent to pilot's and co-pilot's throttles. A wing flap position indicator is located on the pilot's instrument panel.

1-7.6 Artificial Feel - When operating the aileron, rudder, and elevator systems hydraulically, artificial feel is supplied to the control column and pedals proportioned to the speed of the airplane and angular position of the control surface. For further details refer to Chapter 7-6.

1-7.7 Gust Locks - Cylinders of aileron, rudder, and elevator No. 1 systems are provided with hydraulically operated gust locks which lock the actuating cylinder. They are controlled from pilot's pedestal by means of two selector valves connected in series in such a manner that both valves must be in the locked position to lock the surface. If either valve is at UNLOCK the surface will not be locked.

1-7.8 Automatic Pilot - Two complete Pioneer Type P-1 electrically operated automatic pilots are provided. One is designated "Auto Pilot" and operates the main control surfaces through the hydraulic boosters. The other is referred to as "Auto Flying Tab" (Auto FT) and operates the flying tab surfaces directly. A formation stick controller located on the left side of the pilot's seat is used for both "Auto Pilot" and "Auto Flying Tab" control.

PILOTS INSTRUMENT PANEL

1-8 INSTRUMENTS -

1-8.1 Pilot's Station Flight Instruments - The pilot's instrument panel is mounted under the port windshield, forward of the control wheel and directly in front of the pilot's seat. Pointers, numerals, and main graduations on instrument dials are yellow fluorescent coated and become illuminated under fluorescent lighting. The panel is supported by two brackets attached to the floor and is made up of the following instruments:

(a) One direct reading magnetic compass with appropriate deviation card.

(b) Two Kollsman sensitive airspeed indicators supplied from pitot tubes and static taps on the side of the airplane.

(c) Two Pioneer gyroscopic turn and bank indicators, one a component of the automatic pilot and one a component of the auto flying tab system.

(d) One differential pressure rate of climb indicator supplied from a static tap on the side of the airplane.

(e) Two remote indicating gyro flux-gate compasses, one a component of the automatic pilot and one a component of the auto flying tab system. An electrical caging mechanism in the remote compass transmitter is synchronized with the manual caging mechanism in the vertical gyro control to make sure that the gyros in both instruments go through the caging and uncaging cycle together. Turning the manual caging knob on the vertical gyro control automatically operates the electrical caging circuit. In addition, caging or uncaging the gyros controls the operation of a solenoid in the clutch switch which not only disengages the automatic pilot whenever the caging cycle starts but also prevents re-engagement until the gyros are uncaged.

(f) Two Pioneer gyro horizons (vertical gyro control), each a component of the two auto pilot systems.

(g) One yaw meter operated by an external autosyn transmitter located on top of the airplane.

(h) One Sperry vacuum driven gyro trim indicator. 26V inverter switches located on flight engineer's electrical panel automatically turn on the electrically driven vacuum pump.

(i) One eight-day windup clock.

(j) One Bendix radio compass with a red and green range.

(k) Two pressure type altimeters.

(l) Aileron, rudder, and elevator - surface, trim tab, and flying tab position indicators.

(m) Flap position indicators.

(n) Strain gauge indicator lights.

(o) Cabin air and outside air temperature gauges.

(p) Airways outer and inner marker beacon lights.

(q) Hydraulic valve jam warning lights.

1-8.2 Copilot's Station Flight Instruments - The copilot's instrument panel is located on the starboard side and is mounted in the same manner as the pilot's instrument panel. The copilot's instrument panel is made up of the following instruments:

(a) One pressure type altimeter.

(b) One airspeed indicator.

(c) One rate of climb indicator.

(d) One gyro flux-gate compass repeater indicator.

(e) One gyro horizon.

(f) One eight-day windup clock.

(g) Flap position indicator.

(h) Aileron, rudder, and elevator trim tab position indicators.

(i) Strain gauge lights.

(j) Turn and bank indicator.

(k) Aileron and elevator trim tab misalignment indicator.

1-8.3 Pilots' Engine Instruments - Located forward of pilots' pedestal between pilot's and copilot's instrument panels and supported by four shock mounts is an engine instrument panel for the use of both pilots. The instruments include the following:

(a) Four dual tachometers.

(b) Four dual manifold pressure indicators.

(c) Four dual torque indicators.

1-8.4 Pilots' Hydraulic Pressure Gauges - Located in front of the pilots' engine instrument panel and attached to the pilots' pedestal is a small panel containing four hydraulic pressure gauges which indicate the pressure in the main and auxiliary hydraulic systems.

1-8.5 Pilots' Overhead Panel - The pilots' overhead panel is attached to the hull ceiling and is centered over the control pedestal. The panel is made up of the following switches and indicator lights:

(a) External doors open warning light.
(b) Four landing light switches.
(c) Dome light switch.
(d) Position light switch.
(e) Anchor light switch.
(f) Pitot heater switch.
(g) Indicator lights intensity switch.
(h) Bailout signal switch.
(i) Fire warning lights.
(j) Flare release switch.
(k) Flare selector switches.
(l) Indicator light test switch.

1-8.6 Flight Engineer's Instruments - The flight engineer's station is considered the nerve center of the airplane as the flight engineer is able to operate all equipment in the airplane except the flight controls. The operational systems are simplified for the flight engineer through the use of many automatic control systems and warning lights. The instruments and controls are arranged in composite grouping so that all instruments are closely related to the controls whose operation they reflect and that the controls are in position for logical sequence of operation.

(a) Flight Engineer's Engine Panel - This portion of the flight engineer's station is on the starboard side directly behind the copilot's seat and faces inboard. The eight banks of controls and instruments are numbered from left to right (1-8 inclusive) for each engine. The following switches, indicator lights, and instruments are located on this panel:

1. Eight oil pressure gauges.
2. Eight oil pressure low, warning lights.
3. Eight oil dilution switches (inoperative).
4. Eight oil temperature gauges.
5. Eight oil flap open, switches.
6. Eight oil flap position indicators.
7. Eight oil flap control switches.
8. Eight carburetor air temp gauges with indicator light and control switch for each gauge.

9. Carburetor air lights test switch.
10. Eight fuel pressure gauges.
11. Eight fuel pressure low, warning lights.
12. Eight fuel flow gauges.
13. Free air temperature gauge.
14. Eight cylinder head temperature gauges with high temperature warning light for each gauge.
15. Eight mixture control levers.
16. Mixture lights test switch.
17. Pressure type altimeter.
18. Eight cowl flap position indicators and individual switches.
19. Master cowl flap switch.
20. Eight day 24 hour dial clock.
21. Eight manifold pressure gauges.
22. Propeller synchroscope indicator and sensitivity selector switch.
23. Propeller synchroscope master engine selector switch.
24. Eight tachometers.
25. Eight bmep gauges.

(b) Flight Engineer's Oil System Control Panel - This panel is located at the top of the flight engineer's center instrument panel and contains all controls and instruments relative to the engine oil supply and the transfer of oil from the oil reservoir to the nacelle oil tanks as follows:

1. Eight firewall oil valve switches.
2. Eight oil level low, warning lights.
3. Eight nacelle oil tank quantity gauges.
4. Eight oil transfer selector switches.
5. Oil transfer pump on, indicator light.
6. Reserve oil tank quantity gauge.

(c) Flight Engineer's Fuel System Control Panel - This panel is located on the flight engineer's center instrument panel just below the Oil System Panel and contains all controls and instruments required to load fuel aboard the airplane, transfer fuel to the wing tanks and supply fuel to the engines both from the wing tanks and the emergency system. The panel is made up of the following instruments, switches, and indicator lights:

1. Eight firewall fuel valve switches.
2. Four booster pump switches.
3. Four fuel quantity gauges and warning lights.
4. Two fuel tank selector switches.
5. Two transfer pump switches and indicator lights.
6. Fuel pump scavenge switch and indicator light.
7. Several emergency pump selector switches and indicator lights.

8. Several hull tank selector switches and lights.
9. Two fuel loading port selector switches and lights.
10. Indicator selector switch.

(d) Flight Engineer's Electrical Panel - This portion of the flight engineer's station is located aft of flight engineer's seat and faces forward. This panel contains all controls and instruments required to operate the electrical system under normal and emergency conditions. The panel is made up of the following sub-panels with the necessary instruments, switches, and indicator lights to accomplish operation of the various systems concerned.

1. Generator control panel.
2. Dynamotor control panel.
3. Auto pilot, auto flying tab, and inverter control panel.
4. Pneumatic system control panel.
5. Fuel tank CO_2 and ventilator control panel.
6. APU control panel.

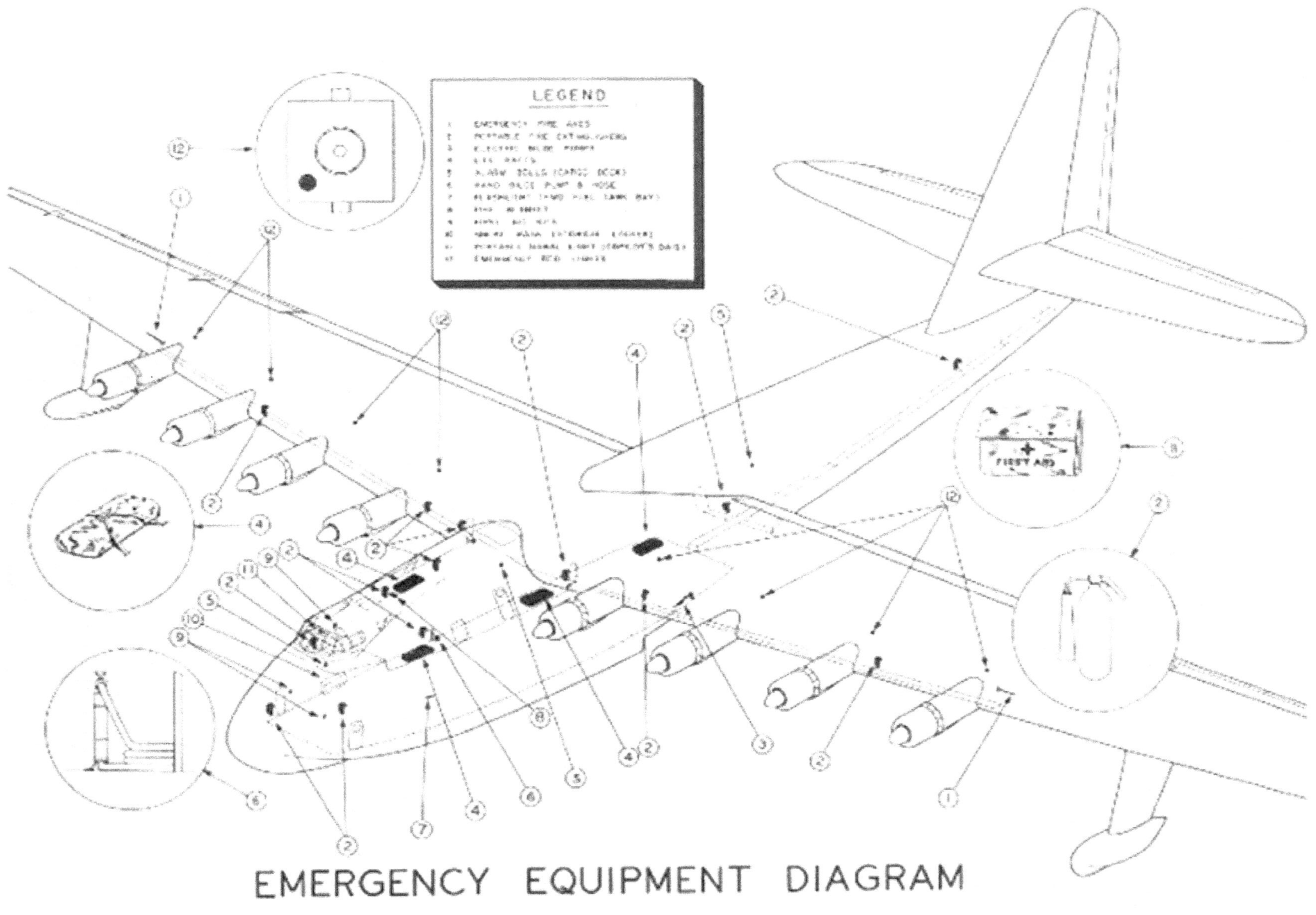

LEGEND
FIRST AID
EMERGENCY EQUIPMENT DIAGRAM

1-9 EMERGENCY EQUIPMENT -

1-9.1 Portable Fire Extinguishers - There are fourteen portable 7-1/2 lb CO_2 hand fire extinguishers located as follows:

1. Aft side of copilot's dais.
2. Front spar of vertical stabilizer.
3. Forward starboard cargo deck access door.
4. Aft starboard cargo deck access door.
5. Auxiliary hydraulic station.
6. Aft flight deck at port wing root.
7. Aft flight deck at starboard wing root.
8. Aft of No. 2 nacelle.
9. Aft of No. 4 nacelle.
10. Aft of No. 5 nacelle.
11. Aft of No. 7 nacelle.
12. Prop test table.
13. Forward of APUs.
14. Forward side of strain gauge table.

1-9.2 Fire Extinguishing System - The fire extinguishing system is composed of six interconnected systems; namely, hull systems A and B, left wing systems A and B, and right wing systems A and B. Thirty six, 50 lb CO_2 cylinders mounted in supporting brackets are located on the cargo deck between stations 899 and 1015. These cylinders are connected through feed lines and valves to strategically located nozzles. CO_2 discharged through these nozzles should effectively smother any fire in the engine, nacelle, wing leading edge, auxiliary power unit, or hull fuel tank areas. A crossfeed valve arrangement is provided to selectively interconnect the six systems, permitting discharge if necessary, of all 36 CO_2 cylinders through a single discharge valve to any selected area, except the APU area which is fed from hull systems A and B, one cylinder at a time. Control switches for the fire extinguishing system and the fire warning lights are located on the flight engineer's electrical and engine panels.

1-9.3 Emergency Red Lights and Alarm Bells - There is one emergency red light located behind each engine nacelle and three alarm bells distributed along the starboard side of the cargo deck. These lights and bells are used as the signal to abandon airplane, and the switch for their operation is located on the pilot's overhead instrument panel.

1-9.4 Fire Axes - Two fire axes are located as follows:

1. Port wing front spar and outboard of No. 1 nacelle.
2. Starboard wing front spar and outboard of No. 8 nacelle.

1-9.5 Life Rafts -

1. Aft of emergency exit on starboard side of flight deck.
2. Forward of emergency exit on port side of flight deck.
3. Aft of rear access door on port side of flight deck.
4. Aft cargo deck.

NOTE

Life rafts should be inflated outside the airplane by pulling sharply on the lanyard to the CO_2 bottle.

1-9.6 First Aid Kits -

1. Aft of forward access door on starboard side of cargo deck.
2. At flight engineer's station.

1-9.7 Signal Light - A portable sealed beam signal light is stowed on the rear of the co-pilot's seat. Another is stored in locker on starboard side of cargo deck.

1-9.8 Parachutes - It will be the responsibility of each crew member to stow his parachute in an accessible place.

1-9.9 Life Vests - It will be the responsibility of each crew member to stow his life vest in an accessible place.

1-9.10 Electric Bilge Pumps and Hose - On the port side of rear cargo deck there are two fixed electric bilge pumps with a capacity of 180 gallons a minute each, and equipped with sufficient length of hose to reach all bilge areas.

1-9.11 Hand Bilge Pump and Hose - Located aft of companionway on starboard side of cargo deck is a portable hand operated bilge pump and suction hose.

1-9.12 Smoke Mask - A smoke mask is stowed in the stowage compartment located on starboard side of cargo deck aft of forward access door.

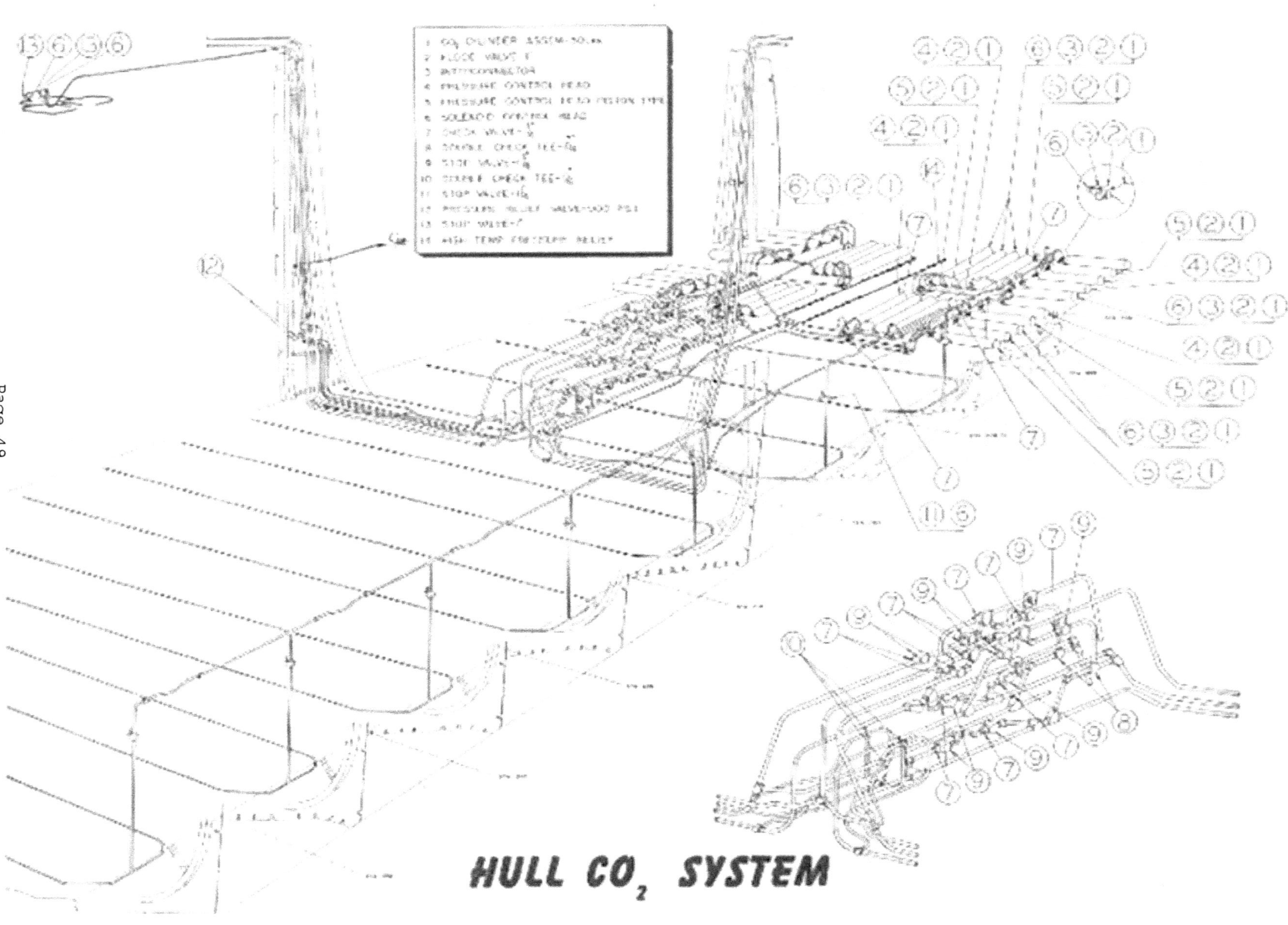
HULL CO_2 SYSTEM

WING CO_2 SYSTEM

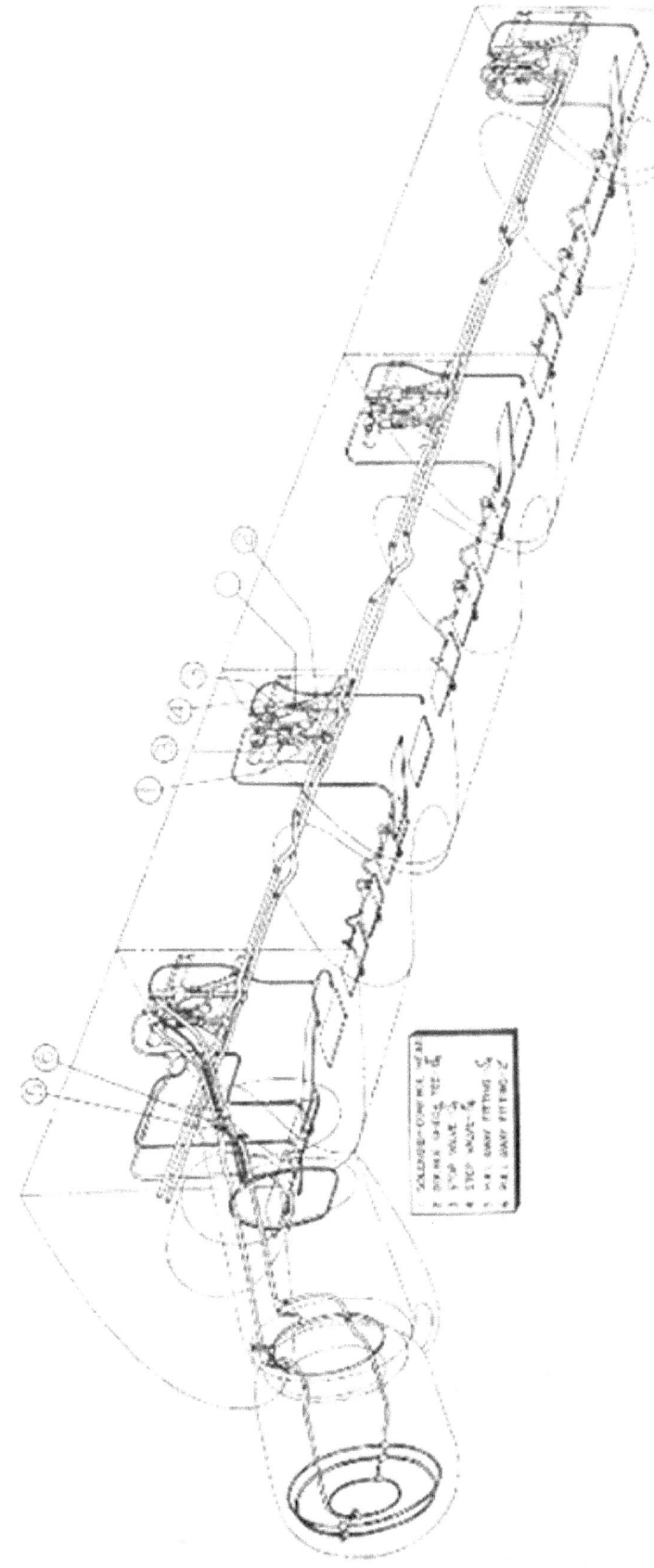

1-10 HATCHES AND DOORS -

1-10.1 Cargo Deck Doors - Four cargo deck access doors are provided, one forward and one aft of the wing on each side of the airplane. The doors open outward and are equipped with emergency release handles and operating instructions stenciled near the handle. Normal access to the airplane is through the aft cargo deck doors. The port forward access door is used for handling the anchor and bow mooring cable. Access to the empennage is through the empennage inspection doors located at aft end of cargo deck. A warning light located on pilot's overhead instrument panel is provided to indicate when external doors are not latched.

1-10.2 Flight Deck Doors - Entrance to the flight deck is normally by way of the companionway from the cargo deck; however, entrance to the flight deck from the outside may be accomplished through the two aft flight deck doors. Entrance to the wing leading edge passageway is by way of the wing access doors located on each side of the aft flight deck. There are two forward flight deck emergency exits which will jettison when opened.

1-10.3 Hatches - There is a flight deck hatch located in the aft flight deck ceiling which may be used for access to the topside wing walkway or as a crash exit. Hatches are located over pilot's and copilot's stations and are to be used as crash exits only.

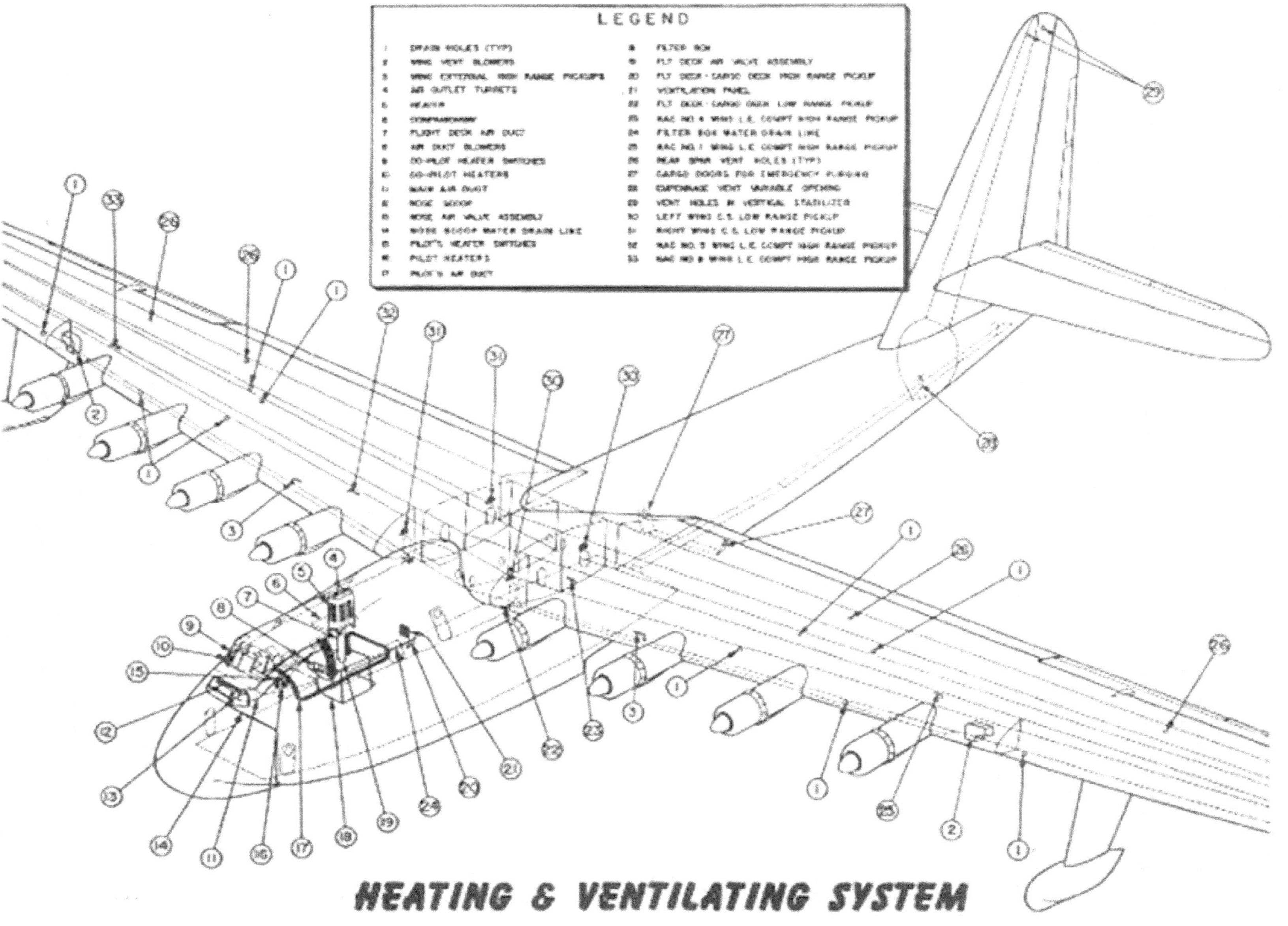
LEGEND
1 DRAIN HOLES (TYP)
2 WING VENT BLOWERS
3 WING EXTERNAL HIGH RANGE PICKUPS
4 AIR OUTLET TURRETS
5 HEATER
6 COMPANIONWAY
7 FLIGHT DECK AIR DUCT
8 AIR DUCT BLOWERS
9 CO-PILOT HEATER SWITCHES
10 CO-PILOT HEATERS
11 MAIN AIR DUCT
12 NOSE SCOOP
13 NOSE AIR VALVE ASSEMBLY
14 NOSE SCOOP WATER DRAIN LINE
15 PILOT'S HEATER SWITCHES
16 PILOT HEATERS
17 PILOT'S AIR DUCT
18 FILTER BOX
19 FLT DECK AIR VALVE ASSEMBLY
20 FLT DECK - CARGO DECK HIGH RANGE PICKUP
21 VENTILATION PANEL
22 FLT DECK - CARGO DECK LOW RANGE PICKUP
23 NAC NO 4 WING L.E. COMPT HIGH RANGE PICKUP
24 FILTER BOX WATER DRAIN LINE
25 NAC NO 1 WING L.E. COMPT HIGH RANGE PICKUP
26 REAR SPAR VENT HOLES (TYP)
27 CARGO DOORS FOR EMERGENCY PURGING
28 EMPENNAGE VENT VARIABLE OPENING
29 VENT HOLES IN VERTICAL STABILIZER
30 LEFT WING C.S. LOW RANGE PICKUP
31 RIGHT WING C.S. LOW RANGE PICKUP
32 NAC NO. 5 WING L.E. COMPT HIGH RANGE PICKUP
33 NAC NO 8 WING L.E. COMPT HIGH RANGE PICKUP
HEATING & VENTILATING SYSTEM

1-11 AUXILIARY SYSTEMS AND EQUIPMENT -

1-11.1 Heating and Ventilating System - This system controls airflow (heated if necessary) through the airplane. Air enters through a nose scoop located just forward of the windshield, then is ducted aft through parallel blowers into the filter box located below the companionway door on the cargo deck. From the filter box, a portion of the flow goes to the pilot's fresh air tube and the remainder passes through the heater to the flight deck. After circulating through the flight deck, the air is discharged through the wing leading edge access doors and through the companionway door into the cargo deck. The air is exhausted from the wing leading edge through the drain holes located forward of the front spar and through the wing leading edge blower outlets. The cargo deck air is discharged through a remotely controlled valve in the empennage door and through the various openings in the wing intermediate and trailing edge sections. Primary controls for the heating and ventilating system are located on the assistant flight engineer's control panel. Wing leading edge blower override controls are located on the flight engineer's engine panel. A switch located at the pilot's station controlling the flight deck valve allows the pilot to restrict the airflow to the flight deck as desired.

Variation and airflow quantities and directions are possible for emergency or other specific requirements by manipulating the following:

(a) Main duct valve located between scoop and blowers.
(b) Flight deck duct valve located in outlet of filter box.
(c) Companionway door (normally open).
(d) Wing leading edge access door (butterfly valve normally open).
(e) Empennage door vent (remotely controlled from assistant flight engineer's station).
(f) Aft cargo door vents.
(g) Main blowers.
(h) Wing leading edge blowers.

1-11.2 Communications Equipment - All communications equipment operates on power received from the ship's 24V system, except that the compass receivers also require power from the 26V 400 cycle inverters and the 4 HAC interphone amplifiers receive power from the main 120V DC system. The emergency range receiver, located outboard of the pilot's station, can be operated from a 24V dry cell powerpack. The communications equipment installed in the airplane and its use is as follows:

(a) The RTA-1 and ARC-3 command equipment are intended primarily for use by the pilot in maintaining contact with control towers, CAA control and weather stations, and the Hughes flight test tower.

(b) The TA-2 liaison transmitter and RA-1 liaison receiver are normally used by the radio operator for long range communications between the aircraft and ground stations.

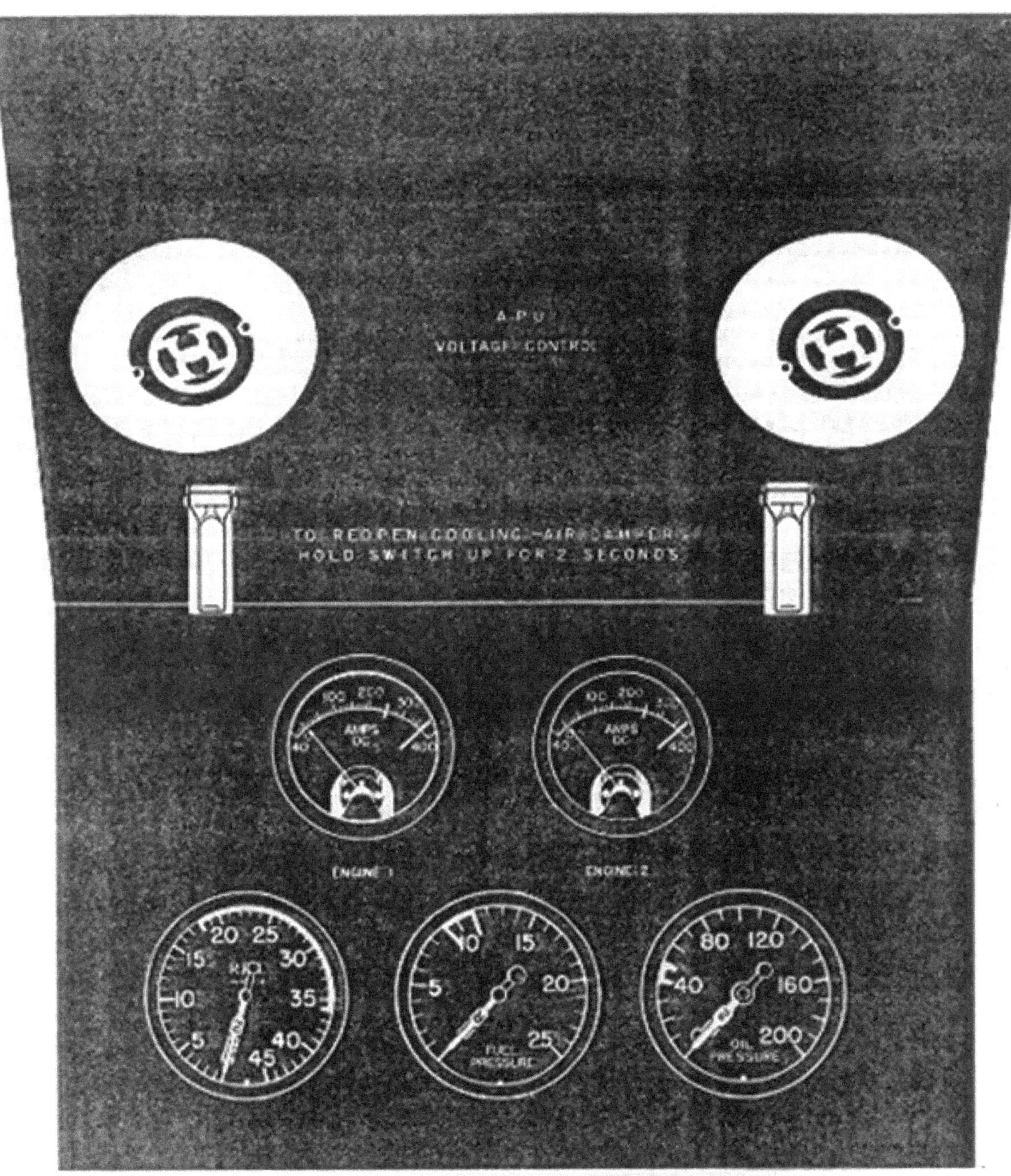

APU INSTRUMENT PANEL

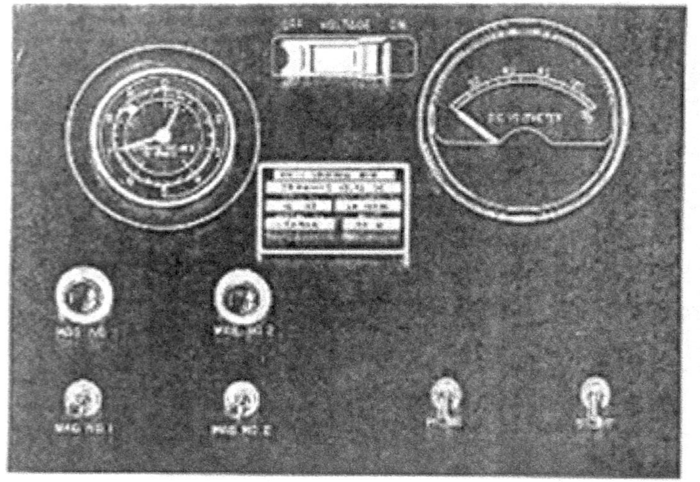

NO.1

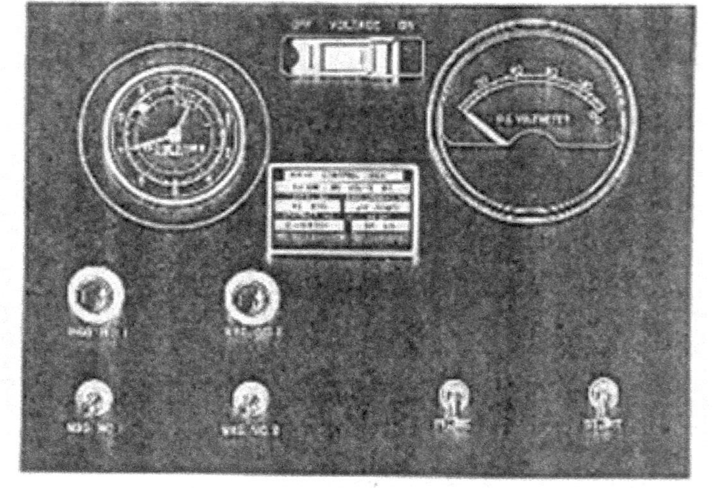

NO.2

APU ELECTRICAL CONTROL PANELS

(c) The SCR-269 compass receivers automatically indicate the bearing from the ship to any station selected by the radio operator. Indicators are located on the pilot's flight instrument panel and the radio operator's panel.

(d) The RA-10 range receivers are intended for receiving low frequency range and control tower stations. The emergency receiver is to be used in case of failure of the 24V DC system.

(e) The MN-53 marker beacon receiver indicates passage over an airways outer or inner marker beacon, audibly by a high pitched tone and visually by three lights on the pilot's instrument panel.

(f) There are 39 airplane interphone stations located throughout the airplane.

(g) The flight deck interphone system has 11 stations on the flight deck and one at the emergency hydraulic station on the cargo deck.

(h) The flight test interphone system has 3 stations located on the flight deck.

1-11.3 Lighting Equipment -

(a) Interior Lights -

1. Dome lights are located in the cargo compartment at stations 353, 475, 597, 782, 1015, and 1262. All these dome lights can be operated by either of two switches, one of which is located aft of the port forward cargo deck access door, the other to the rear of the starboard aft flight deck access door. Each switch operates all lights.

2. There are three entrance lights. One is located on the flight deck, overhead, at the flight engineer's station and the other two are located on the cargo deck, overhead, at stations 230 and 414. These lights are 24V lights and go off automatically when the 120V system is turned on. They may be operated by any one of four switches. One of these switches is located at each of the four cargo deck access doors.

3. Flight deck lights:

a. Two spotlights with switches attached, located on each side of pilot's overhead instrument panel.
b. One dome light over pilot's pedestal. The switch is on pilot's overhead panel.
c. One spotlight over pilot with switch attached.
d. One spotlight over copilot with switch attached.
e. One spotlight and one dome light overhead at station 292 which shines on flight engineer's panel. Each light has its own switch attached to the fixture.

f. One spotlight and one dome light over radio operator. Each light has its own switch attached to the fixture.
g. One dome light over navigator's station with switch on the fixture.
h. One desk lamp with switch attached on the navigation table.
i. One dome light with switch attached, overhead, at station 475.

4. Wing and nacelle dome lights which shine forward and down are mounted overhead on the front spar. There is one light for each nacelle and this lighting is identical in both wings. The switches for operating these lights are located at the entrance to the starboard and port wings.

5. Two console lights are located forward and aft of the throttles. They are recessed into the sides of the flight engineer's station and are shaded to prevent them from shining in the flight engineer's eyes. One switch located above and inboard of the aft console light and marked CONSOLE LIGHT, operates both lights.

6. A spotlight is mounted on top of the cabinet at the auxiliary hydraulic panel. The switch for this goose neck lamp is on the lamp base.

7. There are six empennage dome lights. One is located above and starboard of door on the aft side of the front spar, one over the catwalk on the aft side of the center spar, two over the catwalk on the aft side of the rear spar and two on the aft side of the center spar at vertical station 95. A switch which operates all six lights is mounted on the light fixture which is located on the aft side of the front vertical spar directly over and to the right of the catwalk. The two lights at vertical station 95 have their own switches mounted on their own fixtures, but these lights will not operate unless the main switch is on.

8. There are four aft hull lights which are operated by one switch at aft port cargo deck access door. Two of these lights are located aft of the rear wing spar, overhead, close to the mold line and illuminate the aileron and flap mechanism; the third light is located at station 1568 on starboard side, and the fourth light is at station 2046 on the port side.

(b) Exterior Lights -

1. Two large landing lights are located on the leading edge of each wing between the two inboard nacelles and are controlled by switches on the pilots' overhead panel labeled L WING and R WING.

2. Two small landing lights are located in the leading edge of each float strut and are controlled by switches on the pilots' overhead panel labeled L FLOAT and R FLOAT.

3. Six anchor lights operated by a switch on the pilots' overhead instrument panel are located as follows:

a. One on upper and lower surface of each wing near tip.
b. One on each side of vertical stabilizer near top.

4. Seven position lights operated by a switch on the pilot's overhead panel are located as follows:

   a. One white light on top of hull at station 300.
   b. One white light on the underside of each wing on the inboard flap hinge fairing point.
   c. One red light on the port wing tip.
   d. One green light on the starboard wing tip.
   e. One red and one white in the tail cone.

A flasher selector switch for the position lights is located underneath the main electrical junction box on the front wing spar.

1-11.4 Pneumatic System - Compressed air for supercharging of the hydraulic fluid reservoirs and for the flight deck window seals is supplied by two electrically driven air compressors which constitute the principal portion of a dual pneumatic system referred to as system No. 1 and No. 2. Each system can be operated independently of the other and carry the full load. The pneumatic system control panel is located on the forward cargo deck at the auxiliary hydraulic control station. Pneumatic system control switches and hydraulic reservoir pressure gauges are located on the flight engineer's electrical instrument panel.

1-11.5 Combustible Gas Alarm - A combustible gas alarm continuously analyzes air samples from the hull tank compartments and APU housing for the presence of combustible gases or vapors. An alarm signal is given when the concentration of combustible vapors reaches or exceeds a given percentage below the lower explosive limit (LEL) of the vapor in the air; this alarm signal continues until the necessary attention is given to the conditions that caused the alarm and the instrument is reset. There are 12 indicator lights located on the flight engineer's control panel and a meter type indicator on the detector box panel located on the cargo deck.

1-11.6 Mooring and Anchoring Equipment and Facilities -

(a) Description of Mooring Facilities - The airplane will be secured to the mooring buoy by means of cables connected to the bow towing fitting which is located on the keel at hull station 230. The cables used for this purpose consist of the bow pendant cable and the buoy mooring line. The buoy mooring line is a 5/8" diameter 6 x 19 corrosion resistant cable 50' long, attached to the mooring buoy at one end and provided with a 1" shackle at the free end. There are several sponge floats attached to the buoy mooring line which are used to support the line after the airplane has cast off. The bow pendant line is a 5/8" diameter 6 x 19 corrosion resistant cable 23' 4" long, attached to the airplane by means of the hull bow towing fitting. The free end of this line is provided with a 1-1/2" ID eye. When not in use, the bow pendant line fits snugly into a groove in the bottom of the keel, the forward end being led up through a hole into the interior of the airplane's nose, where it is secured under nominal tension by means of a hook with a threaded shank. There is a 50' length of 1/4" diameter manila rope attached to the eye in the end of the bow pendant line by means of a Coleman hook. This length of manila rope is used for pulling the bow pendant line up into the airplane after it is disconnected from the buoy mooring line. By means of a cable clamp and shackle, a lizard line is attached to the bow pendant line just below the point at which the bow pendant line enters the hole in the keel. This lizard line is a 1/8" diameter 7 x 19 corrosion resistant cable 37' long which leads aft on the outside of the hull to a point just forward of the port forward cargo deck access door where it enters the airplane through a lizard pipe. It is secured inside the airplane by means of a pair of vise wrench hand pliers. The lizard line is used for retrieving the bow pendant line when it is released from its stowage hook in the nose of the airplane. A large safety hook and shackle are provided for making a connection between the bow pendant line and the buoy mooring line. The safety hook and shackle are stowed on the cargo deck floor just forward of the port forward cargo deck door. The shackle and safety hook are attached to the bow pendant line eye after the bow pendant line has been pulled through the port forward cargo deck access door.

(b) Description of Warm Up Facilities - One small boat will be required for connecting the aft towing and warm up cable to the airplane and for disconnecting the bow pendant cable. The aft warm up buoy consists of:

1. One ten ton anchor.
2. One seadrome inner tube type buoy.
3. 150' of 1-1/8" diameter cable and 200' of 1-1/2" diameter anchor chain, to fasten buoy to anchor.
4. 30' of 1" diameter cable is attached to the seadrome buoy. This cable is supported by six plastic floats and on the free end is equipped with a special fitting for tieing up to the airplane's aft towing and warm up hook.

(c) Description of Anchoring Facilities - The anchor is provided as a means of securing the airplane when the mooring buoy is not available. The anchor cable will be secured to the anchor, the anchor dropped to the bottom and the other end of the anchor cable connected to the bow pendant line using the anchor cable grab. A description of the various anchoring facilities follows:

1. Anchor - A Danforth Mark II, 150 pound anchor is stowed in quick release brackets just aft of the port forward cargo deck access door.

2. Anchor Davit - There is a davit and small ratchet type hand winch with 21 feet of 1/8", 7 x 19 steel cable wrapped on the cable drum. This assembly is mounted on the station 230 frame in such a manner that the anchor can be raised from its stowed position and swung through the port forward cargo deck access door.

3. Anchor Winch - The anchor winch consists of a cable drum holding 250 feet of 1/2", 6 x 19 stainless steel cable, and an Eclipse (Model F125989, Type 1408) 120V DC crane hoist unit mounted on the port side of the station 230 bulkhead below the cargo deck floor. An extension shaft for the hand crank and the brake release cable extend up through the cargo deck floor. There is a glass covered inspection port in the cargo deck floor, just above the inboard side of the cable reel. The winch motor control switch is located on the port forward cargo deck access door switch panel and the switch positions are OFF, UP, and DOWN. The anchor cable is led overboard through a hawse pipe located 18" below the center of the top of the port forward cargo deck access door sill.

NOTE

The crane hoist unit gear ratio is 546:1, and the clutch is set at 1167 foot pounds.

4. Anchor Cable Grab - An anchor cable grab is provided for securing the bow pendant line to the anchor cable. The grab is stowed in straps located on the cargo deck floor, just ahead of the left forward access door.

5. Anchor Hoist Crank - The anchor hoist crank may be used to raise the anchor manually if necessary. It is stowed in the stowage compartment located on the starboard side of the cargo deck just aft of the forward cargo deck access door.

6. Sea Anchors - One sea anchor equipped with 125' of 1" manila tow line and 100' of 1/2" manila trip line, is stowed behind each aft cargo deck access door.

7. Pendant Cable Mooring Hook - located on port side of auxiliary hydraulic cabinet on cargo deck.

1-11.7 Miscellaneous -

(a) Chemical Toilet - One located on the aft starboard side of cargo deck and one to be located on the flight deck.

(b) Boat Hooks - There are four boat hooks located as follows:

1. Two located on catwalks aft of rear cargo doors.
2. One at forward starboard cargo deck access door.
3. One at forward port cargo deck access door.

(c) Vacuum Bottles and Drinking Cups - There are two racks for vacuum bottles and two containers for paper cups located as follows:

1. Flight engineer's station.
2. Starboard side of companionway on cargo deck.

(d) Divans - There are two divans that are considered optional equipment and if they are to be used will be located on the port side of forward cargo deck.

(e) Flashlight - One safety type flashlight is stowed below the cargo deck in the forward tank bay.

(f) Ladders - There are two portable ladders stowed on the port side of cargo deck aft of forward access door.

(g) Hand Lanterns (portable battery operated) - Five portable battery operated hand lanterns are located in stowage locker on cargo deck.

(h) Lines - There are several assorted sizes and lengths of line stored as follows:

1. One 1-1/4 inch emergency tow line, 50 feet long, stowed on port line rack.
2. One 1 inch emergency handling line, 60 feet long with a 5 inch loop on each end to fit over snubbing post, stpwed on port line rack.
3. Four 1/4 inch heaving lines, 60 feet long, with weight attached.
4. Two 3/8 inch miscellaneous lines, 100 feet long, stowed on starboard line rack.
5. One 1/2 inch miscellaneous line, 100 feet long with eye on one end, stowed on starboard line rack.
6. One 1-1/4 inch emergency tow line, 50 feet long, stowed on starboard line rack.

(i) Canvas Buckets - Two ten quart canvas buckets are located as follows:

1. Ahead of forward access door on line rack on port side of cargo deck.
2. Ahead of forward access door on line rack on starboard side of cargo deck.

(j) Snubbing Post Yoke - There are two on port line stowage rack and two on starboard line stowage rack on cargo deck.

(k) Grappling Hooks - One stowed on each port and starboard line rack on cargo deck.

(l) Binoculars - One pair in engineer's stowage locker on flight deck.

(m) Safety Belts - Safety belts are installed on all seats.

(n) Snubbing Post Attach Rings - There are four on port line stowage rack and four on starboard line stowage rack. Also, there is a steel tie between the port and starboard snubbing post that must be stowed between the two snubbing post at all times.

(o) Stowage Locker - The following pieces of equipment are stowed in the stowage compartment located on starboard side of cargo deck aft of forward access door:

1. One smoke mask apparatus.
2. Five hand lanterns.
3. One megaphone.
4. One fuel loading valve.
5. Two drop cords.
6. One hand crank for anchor winch.
7. One oil loading hose.
8. One sealed beam signal light.

(p) Extra Light Bulbs and Fuses - These are located in the cabinet above the flight engineer's electrical control panel and junction box.

TABLE OF CONTENTS

SECTION II - NORMAL OPERATING INSTRUCTIONS

(CHECK LISTS)

SECTION II - NORMAL OPERATING INSTRUCTIONS - CHECK LISTS

2-1 BEFORE ENTERING AIRPLANE -

PILOT	ENGINEER
1. See Section V for operating limitations of the airplane.	1. See Section V for operating limitations of the airplane.
2. Flight Plan - Check weather and wind data. Determine amount of fuel, air speed, power settings, etc, necessary for completion of proposed flight with aid of charts in APPENDIX I-OPERATING DATA.	2. Flight Plan - Aid pilot in gathering essential data.
3. Weight and Balance - Obtain the latest weight and balance form from the weight control engineer.	
	4. Exterior Inspection Check - (a) All engine nacelles and propellers to make certain there are no obstructions. (b) Security of cowling and removable panels. (c) All control surfaces to make certain they are clear of all obstructions, and that all access hole covers are installed. (d) Skin and fabric for condition. (e) Liquid leakage - fuel, engine oil, hydraulic oil, etc. (f) All wing tip float access covers installed and wing tip float air cells removed. (g) Underside of flaps for damage.

2-1.1 Access to Airplane - Normal access to the plane is through the aft cargo deck doors. Toggle switches conveniently located adjacent to each of the four cargo deck entrance doors operate the 24V DC hull entrance light system. This system is composed of three lights, one located over the flight engineer's station and two on the cargo deck ceiling. The hull entrance lights become inoperative when the 120V electrical power system is ON.

2-2 ON ENTERING THE AIRPLANE -

PILOT	ENGINEER
1. Check that all persons aboard have proper authorization for the flight.	
2. Check that the airplane is loaded in accordance with the weight and balance form issued for the particular flight that will follow.	
	3. Exterior Inspection Check - (a) Remove pitot tube covers (3). (b) Remove covers from artificial feel venturis. (c) Remove covers from APU exhaust ports. (d) Remove yaw-meter cover.
	4. Interior Inspection Check - Check to see if all items in Emergency Equipment (Chapter 1-9), and Miscellaneous (Paragraph 1-11. 9) are in place.
	5. Check quantities of fuel and oil necessary to successfully complete the flight.
	6. Remove external power plugs located near APU outlets and close covers.

2-3 BEFORE STARTING ENGINES -

PILOT	ENGINEER
1. Preflight Inspection Check -	1. Preflight Inspection Check -
(a) Check preflight inspection reports compiled and signed by inspection and flight and service personnel.	(a) Check preflight inspection reports for completion and date of last preflight (24 hr max. elapsed time unless otherwise approved).
(b) If it is desired to repeat the flying tab system check performed by flight and service personnel refer to 7-6.8 (d) and 4-4.4.	2. Set altimeter and clock.
	3. Secure airplane for run-up. (See 2-3.1)
	4. Pitot covers removed (3).
	5. Remove mechanical locks on flight controls.
	6. All Generator Power switches OFF, (Eng 1, 3, and 7).
	7. Battery control (check voltage).
	(a) 120V batteries, L and R ON. (b) 24V (28V DC) battery switch ON.
8. Ask radio operator to turn interphone power ON.	
	9. Start APU 1 and APU 2. Check voltage before turning on generators. (For starting procedure refer to Chapter 4-5.1)
	10. One 26V Inverter (Inv 1 or Inv 2) on MAIN.
	11. Auto Pilot and Auto FT (flying tab) Inverters on MAIN.
	12. One Dynamotor ON (check voltage).
13. Pilot's pedestal flight controls in following position: (Check control positions with lights.)	
(a) Gust Locks LOCK.	

PILOT	ENGINEER
(b) Hyd Control A - Ail., Rud, and Elev ENG. Hyd Control B - Ail., Rud, and Elev OFF.	
(c) Art (artificial) Feel ENG.	
(d) FT (flying tab) Control - Ail., Rud, and Elev OFF.	
(e) FT (flying tab) - Ail., Rud, and Elev OFF.	
(f) Master changeover switch ON to check lights, then OFF.	
(g) Auto Pilot Power, Clutch Master button and Ail., Rud, Elev clutch switches OFF.	
(h) Auto FT (flying tab) Power OFF, Inverter to SMALL, Clutch Master button OFF, and Ail., Rud, and Elev Clutch switches OFF.	
(i) Auto FT (flying tab) Mechanical Disconnect switches ENG.	
CAUTION	
MECHANICAL DISCONNECT SWITCHES ALWAYS "ENGAGED" EXCEPT IN EMERGENCY. IF FOUND DIS-ENGAGED, RE-ENGAGE MANUALLY AT THE CLUTCH.	
(j) Auto FT (flying tab) Power ON to check lights, then OFF.	
(k) Sys 1 and Sys 2 Hydraulic Change-over levers NEUTRAL, Sys 1 and Sys 2 Hyd Changeover Override valves NEUTRAL.	
(l) Aux Hyd Pumps, Sys 1 and Sys 2 OFF.	
(m) Hyd Shutoff Valves, Sys 1 and Sys 2 Ail., Rud, Elev OFF.	
(n) Master Hyd Shutoff Valves Sys 1 and Sys 2 ON to check lights, then OFF.	
(o) Mast Cyl Valves OFF.	

PILOT	ENGINEER
(p) Cyl By-Pass Valves, Sys 1 and Sys 2 Regular and Alternate, Ail., Rud, Elev NORMAL. (q) Flaps UP, Flap Hydraulics switches, Sys 1 and Sys 2 OFF, and Flap Control switch AUTO.	
	14. Auxiliary Hydraulic System Panel: (a) Lowpressure crossfeed CLOSED. (b) Both air supply valves OPEN. (c) Comp (compressor) crossfeed CLOSED. (d) Window Seal OPEN. (e) Master Switches ON (2).
	15. Fuel and Float Comp Blower Control Panel (located aft of companionway on starboard cargo deck): (a) Fuel and Float Comp Blowers OFF. (b) Float Comp Blowers NORMAL. (c) Fuel Comp Vent Blower NORMAL.
	16. Pneumatic system switches, Sys 1 and Sys 2 AUTO. (Check Hyd Res gauges for 40 to 50 psi.)
	17. Fire Warning Lights - Check both engineer's panel and pilot's overhead warning lights with test switches.
	18. Oil System Control Panel: (a) Firewall Oil Valves OPEN. (b) Check quantity of oil in Nacelle Oil Tanks. (c) Oil Transfer, normally OFF.
	19. Fuel System Control Panel: (a) Firewall Fuel Valves CLOSED. (b) Booster pumps OFF. (c) Wing Tanks FULL.

PILOT	ENGINEER
	(d) Transfer Pumps AUTO. Aux (auxiliary) power OFF. (e) Emergency Pump OFF. Aux (auxiliary) power OFF. (f) Liquidometer Selectors and fuel tank valves set to tanks to be used first. (g) Fuel Pumps Scavenge AUTO. (h) Loading Ports CLOSED. (i) Tank indicator switch NORMAL.
	20. Oil Flaps AUTO.
	21. Carb Air COLD.
	22. Mixture CUT-OFF.
	23. Cowl Flaps 100 percent OPEN.
24. Prop Synch lever full forward Increase RPM. (a) Synchronizer on No. 2 Master. (b) Fixed RPM switch neutral.	
	25. Prop governors HIGH RPM.
26. Throttles CLOSED. (a) Throttle transfer switches to ENGINEER, (Flight Eng Vernier OFF). (b) Throttle Control switches AUTO.	
	27. Engineer's throttles CLOSED.
	28. Ignition OFF.
	29. De-Hyd Selector switch positioned as required.
	30. Pull engines through 4 revolutions (8 blades).

2-3.1 Securing Airplane for Warm Up -

(a) Two men will be stationed at the port forward cargo deck access door:

1. One man at the interphone.

2. One man to handle the mooring lines.

(b) Two men will be stationed at the aft towing and warm up hook:

1. One man at the interphone on the aft face of the vertical stabilizer front spar.

2. One man to operate the aft towing and warm up hook.

a. Retract spring loaded bolts at the forward and aft ends of the walkway movable section. Slide walkway toward the starboard side until it hits the stops.

b. At the keel, just aft of the vertical stabilizer front spar, unfasten the four dzus fasteners that hold the cover plate in the closed position.

c. Raise the cover to expose the hook.

d. Pull the trip lever aft to release the hook.

(c) Two boats will be used as follows:

1. One sea mule to be used to tow the airplane.

2. One personnel boat to be used for maneuvering close to the airplane and controlling the airplane's stern.

3. Both boats to be equipped with radios.

(d) The pilot or an assigned crew member equipped with an airplane interphone will take a position atop the observation tower which projects through the escape hatch above the crew deck.

(e) The pilot or crew member atop this observation tower will be in charge of moving the airplane to the warm up position:

1. Have the sea mule position itself approximately 100' in front of the Hughes Flying Boat. On board the sea mule is 150' of 2" diameter manila rope. The free end of the rope will have a 6" ring attached to it.

2. Advise the personnel boat to pick up the free end of the 2" diameter manila rope and carry it to the bow mooring pendant hook.

3. Have crew member disconnect the mooring buoy cable from the bow mooring pendant hook and snap the 6" ring attached to the free end of the 2" diameter manila rope onto the hook.

4. Advise the sea mule to take up the slack in the 2" diameter manila rope and hold the airplane into the wind until further orders.

5. Advise personnel boat to pick the free end of the buoy cable out of the water and prepare to attach it to the stern hook.

6. Advise sea mule to tow the airplane slowly forward passing close to one side of the mooring buoy.

NOTE

Do not tow faster than 1-1/2 knots.

7. As the airplane passes the mooring buoy the personnel boat will attach the buoy cable to the stern hook.

   a. The personnel boat crew member will now slip the ring which is on the end of the buoy cable, over the hook and push the hook closed.

   b. The man inside the airplane should hold the trip lever aft until the hook has been pushed closed and then allow it to spring forward to the locked position.

(f) Notify man atop the observation tower that the airplane is secured both fore and aft and towing may be continued to the warm up position to windward of buoy.

(g) Personnel boat will notify the sea mule when the stern cable is taut.

(h) The sea mule is to maintain a forward pull so as to keep the airplane headed into the wind until one engine has been started.

(i) Stow the bow pendant line.

1. Pull the bow pendant line thru the port forward cargo deck access door with the 1/8" diameter lizard line.

2. Remove the hook and link.

3. Attach the 1/4" diameter manila rope.

4. Drop the bow pendant line over the side.

AVOID CONTACT WITH THE AIRPLANE.

5. Pull the eye on the end of the bow pendant line into the bow of the airplane with the 1/4" diameter manila rope.

6. Lift the eye over the securing hook and turn the wing nut down until the cable is snug.

7. Install the rubber plug in the hole thru which the bow mooring line passes.

8. Coil and stow the 1/4" diameter manila rope.

9. Pull the lizard line in thru the lizard pipe until it is snug.

10. Secure the lizard line with the vise-grip pliers and stow the slack line.

11. Notify the pilot that the bow pendant line is stowed.

2-4 STARTING ENGINES -

PILOT	ENGINEER
1. Starting Sequence - Notify engineer order in which engines are to be started. (a) Wind direction and mooring position will influence starting sequence. (b) If conditions require it, the pilot may take over throttles as engines are started.	
	2. Starting Procedure - (a) Throttles 1/8 OPEN on engine to be started. (800 rpm after start.) (b) Firewall Fuel Valve NORMAL for engine to be started. (c) Booster pump ON for engine to be started. (d) Ignition ON. (c) Crank and PRIME simultaneously to start. (f) Mixture RICH as soon as engine fires regularly on prime. (g) Oil pressure should register almost immediately. (h) Booster pumps OFF. 3. Repeat Starting Procedure for remaining engines.
4. Order personnel boat to remove all lines and clear area ahead of airplane.	

2-5 ENGINE WARM-UP -

PILOT	ENGINEER
	1. Engines - Warm-up at approximately 800 rpm.
2. Flight Control Check - For flight control operational check procedure, refer to card located at flight stations or see 7-6.8 and 4-4.2. Upon completion of this check the hydraulic flight control systems must be ON.	
	3. Emergency Fuel System - (a) Emergency Pump ON. Check that each engine will run on this system for two minutes. (b) Check operation on auxiliary power.
	4. Propeller Governors - Exercise propellers when oil temperature is at least 40°C.
5. Pilot's Prop Controls - (a) Exercise prop synchronizers with Prop Synch lever and Mom (momentary) switches.	
	6. Power Check - Engine speeds in low pitch should be approximately 2400 rpm with Throttles set at MP equal to local barometric pressure. (a) Oil pressure 85-90 psi at 2000 rpm and 75°C. (b) Fuel pressure 25 ± 1 psi at 2000 rpm. **NOTE** If engine run-up is made on warm up hook do not run more than 2 symmetrically located engines to 2400 rpm.

2-6 CASTING OFF -

PILOT	ENGINEER
1. Order stern cable released.	1. Crew member will release stern cable. (a) Pull the trip lever releasing the airplane from the aft mooring line. (b) Crew member will notify pilot that the aft hook is free.
2. Receive clearance from control tower to taxi.	
	3. Crew member will secure aft towing and warm up hook. (a) Reach thru hook access hole in keel and pull the hook to the closed position. (b) Pull the trip lever aft to receive the hook and then forward to lock it. (c) Close the hook cover plate. (d) Fasten the four dzus studs. (e) Slide the walkway section to the airplane center line and lock it with the two spring loaded studs.
	4. Stow all lines and equipment.

2-7 TAXIING -

PILOT	ENGINEER
1. Gustlocks UNLOCK, controls free.	
2. Gyros UNCAGED.	
	3. APUs OFF.
	NOTE Engine speeds below 1450 rpm should not be used for periods of more than 15 minutes duration unless the APUs are in operation. Continuous operation at lower engine speeds will result in discharging the storage batteries unless the APUs are operating and carrying the electrical load.
	4. Engine Generator Power ON (Eng 1, 3, and 7).
	5. Engine Operating Limits - RPM 2550 BMEP 178 Cyl Head Temp 232°C
	6. One Air Duct Blower ON.
	7. Bilge Water Check - The bilges will be checked for water after each fast taxi run and each landing. One crew member will enter the bilge compartments and make a visual inspection for the presence of any water.

PILOT	ENGINEER
NOTE Taxi operations above hump speed should be conducted at a trim angle of 4°.	**WARNING** BE SURE TO USE A SAFETY TYPE FLASHLIGHT FOR ALL WORK BELOW THE CARGO DECK FLOOR. BE SURE TO CLOSE ALL DOORS AFTER LEAVING EACH COMPARTMENT.

2-8 BEFORE TAKEOFF

PILOT	ENGINEER
1. Flight control switches and valves should be in following positions with 2000 lbs hydraulic pressure on Main Sys 1 and Sys 2.	
(a) Gust locks UNLOCK.	
(b) Hyd Control A - Ail., Rud, Elev ENG, Hyd Control B - Ail., Rud, and Elev OFF.	
(c) Art (artificial) Feel, ENG.	
(d) FT (flying tab) Control - Ail., Rud, Elev OFF.	
(e) FT (flying tab) - Ail., Rud, Elev OFF.	
(f) Master changeover switch ON to check lights, then OFF.	
(g) Auto Pilot Power, Clutch Master button, and Ail., Rud, Elev Clutch switches OFF.	
(h) Auto FT (flying tab) Power OFF, inverter to SMALL, Clutch Master button OFF and Ail., Rud, and Elev Clutch switches OFF.	
(i) Auto FT (flying tab) Mechanical Disconnect switches ENG.	
(j) Controller Selector on AUTO FT.	
(k) Gyro switch OUT.	
(l) Sys 1 and Sys 2 Hydraulic Changeover levers MAIN, and Sys 1 and Sys 2 Hyd Changeover Override valves NEUTRAL.	
(m) Aux Hyd Pumps, Sys 1 and Sys 2 OFF.	
(n) Hyd Shutoff Valves - Sys 1 and Sys 2 Ail., Rud, Elev, ON.	
(o) Master Hyd Shutoff Valves Sys 1 and Sys 2 OFF.	
(p) Hand-Pump Hyd System - Regular and Alternate Press 1950 lbs min.	
(q) Mast Cyl Valves OFF.	
(r) Cyl By-Pass Valves Sys 1 and Sys 2, Regular and Alternate, Ail., Rud, Elev NORMAL.	

PILOT	ENGINEER
(a) Flap Hydraulics switch - Sys 2 ON, Sys 1 OFF. Flap Control switch AUTO.	
	2. Hand-Pump Hyd System Shutoff Valves CLOSED (at hand-pump reservoir).
	3. Firewall Fuel Valves NORMAL.
	4. Booster pumps ON.
	5. Wing Tanks FULL.
	6. Transfer Pumps on AUTO.
	7. Emergency Pump OFF.
	(a) No. 8 emergency tank OPEN.
	8. Hull Tanks - proper tanks ON.
	9. Oil Flaps AUTO.
	10. Carb Air COLD.
	11. Mixture RICH.
	12. Cowl Flaps 25 percent OPEN.
	13. Props 2550 rpm.
	14. Transfer Throttles to pilot's control.
15. Throttle Transfer switches to PILOT.	
	16. Hyd Res 1 and Hyd Res 2 supercharged with 40 to 50 lbs air press.
17. Prop Synch (synchronizer) Lever full forward (increase rpm) Synchronizer on No. 2 Master, and Fixed RPM switch neutral.	
18. Flaps 20°.	

PILOT	ENGINEER
19. Trim tabs as required for takeoff. (See Trim Track Chart)	
20. Set altimeter and clock.	
21. Gyros UNCAGED.	
22. Receive takeoff clearance from radio operator.	
23. ALL windows and hatches secure. (Check External Doors indicator light).	
	24. Cargo Deck and Bilge Section - (a) Check with mechanic on cargo deck and be sure all hatches are closed and crew ready for takeoff. (b) Fuel compartment vent valves to flight position and covers on openings in deck.
	25. Check with asst flight engineer's station to see if clear for takeoff.
	26. Note time of takeoff.

2-9 TAKEOFF -

2-9.1 Hydrodynamic Performance Characteristics - The techniques to be employed in handling the airplane while waterborne during takeoff are discussed in detail in Chapter 6-4, which also includes a discussion of hydrodynamic instabilities.

2-9.2 Takeoff Procedure -

(a) Maintain zero degree elevator until beyond hump speed, 58-64 mph (50-55 knots).
(b) When the planing phase is well established gradually apply 5° nose-up elevator.
(c) Hold 5° up elevator until flying speed (at corresponding trim) is attained.

NOTE

Getaway speeds vary between 70-110 mph (61-95 knots) depending upon gross weight, CG, trim, temp, and headwind (see takeoff charts).

2-9.3 Takeoff at Maximum Gross Weights Accompanied by High Ambient Temperatures -

(a) Hold 5° down elevator when approaching and passing hump speed, 34-51 mph (30-45 knots).
(b) Raise nose (0° elevator) after hump speed is passed.
(c) When the planing phase is well established, gradually apply 5° nose-up elevator.
(d) Hold 5° up elevator until flying speed is reached.

PILOT	ENGINEER
1. Advance throttles to takeoff power (49.5" hg - 202 bmep) and adjust throttle friction. Max. operating time at takeoff power is 5 minutes.	
2. Propellers 2550 rpm.	
	3. Engine Operating Limits - Manifold Pressure 49.5. RPM 2550 BMEP 202. Oil pressure 80 to 100 psi. Oil temperature 40° - 85° (98°C max.)

PILOT	ENGINEER
CAUTION A FULLY SUBMERGED TIP FLOAT WILL PULL OFF AT 35 MPH (30 KNOTS).	Carburetor air temperature 38°C max. Fuel pressure 25 ± 1 psi. Cylinder head temperature 232°C max., 195° ± 5°C (desired).

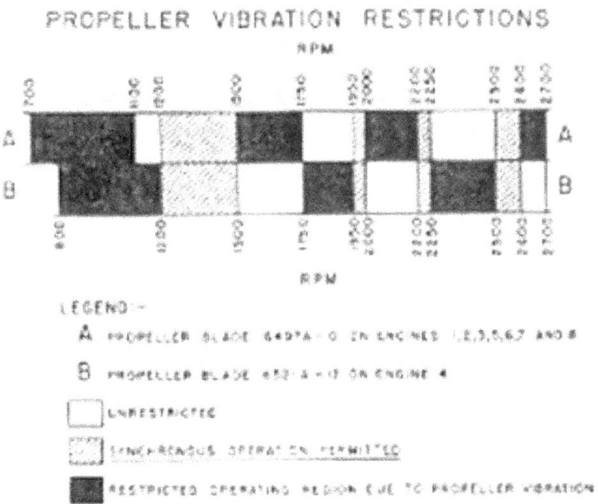

2-10 CLIMB -

PILOT	ENGINEER
1. Props 2550 rpm.	
2. BMEP 176.	
3. Flaps - gradually raise at safe altitude.	
	4. Mixture RICH.
	5. Cowl Flaps - CLOSE as cylinder temperatures permit.
	6. Engine Operating Limits - Oil Pressure 85 - 90 psi. Oil Temperature 60° - 75° desired (98°C max for 5 min). Carburetor Air Temperature 38°C max. Fuel Pressure 25 ± 1 psi. Cylinder Head Temperature 232°C max.

2-11 DURING FLIGHT -

2-11.1 Flight Characteristics - Discussion of flight characteristics is found in Chapter 6-5.

PILOT	ENGINEER
1. Level off at the desired altitude and direct flight engineer to reduce power as required.	
2. Throttle Transfer switches to ENGINEER (if desired).	2. Assume control of Throttles (as directed by pilot).
3. Establish cruise power.	3. Establish cruise power.
4. Trim airplane for level flight.	
	5. Adjust Cowl Flaps as necessary to maintain proper cylinder head temperatures.
	6. Engine Operating Limits - Oil pressure above 2000 rpm - 80 psi. Oil pressure above 1600 rpm - 65 psi. Oil Temp 85°C. Cyl Head Temp 218°C. Fuel pressure 25 ± 1 psi. Carb Air Temp 38°C to 10,000 ft. Carb Air Temp 15°C above 10,000 ft.

NOTE

In order to maintain engine generator load capacity it is necessary to operate engines at speeds above 1450 rpm at all times during flight. For maximum range and endurance cruise, refer to Cruise Charts. Engine generator speed limitations do not permit maximum economy cruising over the entire range of gross weights.

B M E P POWER SETTINGS

HIGH POWER AUTO-RICH

[illegible]

[illegible]

202 BMEP

RPM	ALT (FT)	Manifold Pressure at Carb Air Temp A	B	C	D	Fuel Flow LBS/HR	% Rated Power
[illegible]	S.L. [illegible]	[illegible]	[illegible]	[illegible]		[illegible]	[illegible]
[illegible]	S.L. [illegible]	[illegible]	[illegible]	[illegible]		[illegible]	[illegible]
[illegible]	S.L. [illegible]	[illegible]	[illegible]			[illegible]	[illegible]
[illegible]	S.L. [illegible]	[illegible]	[illegible]			[illegible]	[illegible]

195 BMEP

RPM	ALT (FT)	Manifold Pressure at Carb Air Temp A	B	C	D	Fuel Flow LBS/HR	% Rated Power
[illegible]	S.L. [illegible]	[illegible]	[illegible]	[illegible]	[illegible]	[illegible]	[illegible]
[illegible]	S.L. [illegible]	[illegible]	[illegible]	[illegible]		[illegible]	[illegible]
[illegible]	S.L. [illegible]	[illegible]	[illegible]	[illegible]		[illegible]	[illegible]
[illegible]	S.L. [illegible]	[illegible]	[illegible]	[illegible]		[illegible]	[illegible]

183 BMEP

RPM	ALT (FT)	Manifold Pressure at Carb Air Temp A	B	C	D	Fuel Flow LBS/HR	% Rated Power
[illegible]	S.L. [illegible]	[illegible]	[illegible]	[illegible]	[illegible]	[illegible]	[illegible]
[illegible]	S.L. [illegible]	[illegible]	[illegible]	[illegible]	[illegible]	[illegible]	[illegible]
[illegible]	S.L. [illegible]	[illegible]	[illegible]	[illegible]	[illegible]	[illegible]	[illegible]
[illegible]	S.L. [illegible]	[illegible]	[illegible]	[illegible]	[illegible]	[illegible]	[illegible]

178 BMEP

RPM	ALT (FT)	Manifold Pressure at Carb Air Temp A	B	C	D	Fuel Flow LBS/HR	% Rated Power
[illegible]	S.L. [illegible]	[illegible]	[illegible]	[illegible]	[illegible]	[illegible]	[illegible]
[illegible]	S.L. [illegible]	[illegible]	[illegible]	[illegible]	[illegible]	[illegible]	[illegible]
[illegible]	S.L. [illegible]	[illegible]	[illegible]	[illegible]	[illegible]	[illegible]	[illegible]
[illegible]	S.L. [illegible]	[illegible]	[illegible]	[illegible]	[illegible]	[illegible]	[illegible]
[illegible]	S.L. [illegible]	[illegible]	[illegible]	[illegible]	[illegible]	[illegible]	[illegible]
[illegible]	S.L. [illegible]	[illegible]	[illegible]	[illegible]	[illegible]	[illegible]	[illegible]
[illegible]	S.L. [illegible]	[illegible]	[illegible]	[illegible]	[illegible]	[illegible]	[illegible]
[illegible]	S.L. [illegible]	[illegible]	[illegible]	[illegible]	[illegible]	[illegible]	[illegible]
[illegible]	S.L. [illegible]	[illegible]	[illegible]	[illegible]	[illegible]	[illegible]	[illegible]

165 BMEP

RPM	ALT (FT)	Manifold Pressure at Carb Air Temp A	B	C	D	Fuel Flow LBS/HR	% Rated Power
[illegible]	S.L. [illegible]	[illegible]	[illegible]	[illegible]	[illegible]	[illegible]	[illegible]
[illegible]	S.L. [illegible]	[illegible]	[illegible]	[illegible]	[illegible]	[illegible]	[illegible]
[illegible]	S.L. [illegible]	[illegible]	[illegible]	[illegible]	[illegible]	[illegible]	[illegible]
[illegible]	S.L. [illegible]	[illegible]	[illegible]	[illegible]	[illegible]	[illegible]	[illegible]
[illegible]	S.L. [illegible]	[illegible]	[illegible]	[illegible]	[illegible]	[illegible]	[illegible]
[illegible]	S.L. [illegible]	[illegible]	[illegible]	[illegible]	[illegible]	[illegible]	[illegible]
[illegible]	S.L. [illegible]	[illegible]	[illegible]	[illegible]	[illegible]	[illegible]	[illegible]
[illegible]	S.L. [illegible]	[illegible]	[illegible]	[illegible]	[illegible]	[illegible]	[illegible]
[illegible]	S.L. [illegible]	[illegible]	[illegible]	[illegible]	[illegible]	[illegible]	[illegible]

150 BMEP

RPM	ALT (FT)	Manifold Pressure at Carb Air Temp A	B	C	D	Fuel Flow LBS/HR	% Rated Power
[illegible]	S.L. [illegible]	[illegible]	[illegible]	[illegible]	[illegible]	[illegible]	[illegible]
[illegible]	S.L. [illegible]	[illegible]	[illegible]	[illegible]	[illegible]	[illegible]	[illegible]
[illegible]	S.L. [illegible]	[illegible]	[illegible]	[illegible]	[illegible]	[illegible]	[illegible]
[illegible]	S.L. [illegible]	[illegible]	[illegible]	[illegible]	[illegible]	[illegible]	[illegible]
[illegible]	S.L. [illegible]	[illegible]	[illegible]	[illegible]	[illegible]	[illegible]	[illegible]
[illegible]	S.L. [illegible]	[illegible]	[illegible]	[illegible]	[illegible]	[illegible]	[illegible]
[illegible]	S.L. [illegible]	[illegible]	[illegible]	[illegible]	[illegible]	[illegible]	[illegible]
[illegible]	S.L. [illegible]	[illegible]	[illegible]	[illegible]	[illegible]	[illegible]	[illegible]
[illegible]	S.L. [illegible]	[illegible]	[illegible]	[illegible]	[illegible]	[illegible]	[illegible]

NOTES:

1. [illegible]
2. [illegible]
3. [illegible]
4. [illegible]
5. [illegible]
6. [illegible]

ALT (FT)	A	B	C	D
[illegible]	[illegible]	[illegible]	[illegible]	[illegible]

HIGH POWER AUTO-RICH

B M E P POWER SETTINGS

LOW POWER AUTO-RICH

P & W R4360-4A ENGINES

BRAKE MEAN EFFECTIVE PRESSURE (LBS/SQ. IN.)

RPM	152 BMEP* ALT (FT)	MANIFOLD PRESSURE AT CARB AIR TEMP A	B	C	D	FUEL FLOW LB/HR	RATED POWER (%)
1950	S.L. 5,000 5,500	33.8 32.8 31.3	34.2 33.3 32.5	34.5 33.5	35.4 34.3	750 686	64% 1600
1900	S.L. 5,000 6,100	32.8 31.8 31.1	33.6 32.6 32.1	34.3 33.3	35.2 34.1	748 712	63% 1575
1850	S.L. 5,000 5,800	32.6 31.5 31.0	33.6 32.5 32.0	34.1 33.0	34.9 33.8	734 682	61% 1525
1800	S.L. 5,500 7,400	32.5 31.3 30.8	33.5 32.3 31.8	34.0 32.8	34.8 33.6	725 665	59% 1475
1700	S.L. 4,500	31.8 30.7	32.8 31.6	33.3	34.1	592 536	55% 1250
1650	S.L. 3,900	31.7 30.7	32.7 31.6	33.2	34.0	573 519	49% 1230
1600	S.L. 3,400	31.5 30.6	32.5 31.4	33.0	31.6	555 525	46% 1152

RPM	146 BMEP** ALT (FT)	MANIFOLD PRESSURE AT CARB AIR TEMP A	B	C	D	FUEL FLOW LB/HR	RATED POWER (%)
1950	S.L. 5,000 10,500 12,500	31.3 30.4 29.4 29.1	32.1 31.1 30.6 30.2	32.3 31.4	33.0 32.6	[illegible] 685	60% 1500
1900	S.L. 5,000 10,000 12,200	31.3 30.3 29.5 29.1	32.3 31.2 30.0 29.6	32.7 31.7	33.4 32.4	[illegible] 661	59% 1475
1850	S.L. 6,000 8,400	31.0 30.0 29.9	32.0 31.0 29.4	32.5 31.5	32.3 32.2	708	57% 1425
1800	S.L. 5,200 [illegible]	30.8 29.8 29.4	31.8 30.7 29.4	32.3 31.2	33.1 31.9	686 626	56% 1400
1700	S.L. 5,500 8,900	31.9 29.9 29.3	31.2 29.8 29.2	31.7 32.2	32.6	563 508	46% 1150
1650	S.L. 5,000 8,400	30.2 29.7 29.5	30.3 29.6 29.2	31.6	32.3	544 495	45% 1125
1600	S.L. 5,000 6,800	30.1 29.7 29.9	31.0 29.6 29.3	31.5	32.2	530 476	43% 1075

RPM	131 BMEP** ALT (FT)	MANIFOLD PRESSURE AT CARB AIR TEMP A	B	C	D	FUEL FLOW LB/HR	RATED POWER (%)
1950	S.L. 5,000 11,500 12,500	29.8 28.7 27.7 27.2	30.7 29.6 21.5 28.1	31.2 31.4 28.9	31.3 31.8 28.7	539 641	55% 1400
1900	S.L. 5,000 10,000 12,000	29.9 28.9 27.9 27.2	31.5 29.4 28.4 28.8	31.0 29.6 28.7	31.5 32.8	150 523	54% 1351
1850	S.L. 5,000 10,000 11,100	29.5 28.4 27.4 27.1	31.4 29.5 28.2 27.9	30.8 29.7 28.9	31.5 30.5	533 398	53% 1325
1800	S.L. 5,000 10,000 11,330	29.3 28.2 27.2 27.0	30.2 29.1 28.6 27.8	30.7 29.1	31.4 30.5	567 565	52% 1300
1700	S.L. 5,000 11,000	30.6 29.3 28.9	29.5 29.3 28.9	29.9 28.5	30.2 31.2	535 481	43% 1075
1650	S.L. 5,000 9,500	30.2 27.6 25.9	29.4 27.9 26.5	29.8 28.2	31.4	518 468	42% 1050
1600	S.L. 5,000 9,000	28.4 27.8 25.9	29.6 27.8 26.5	29.7 28.1	30.5	500 452	40% 1000

RPM	120 BMEP** ALT (FT)	MANIFOLD PRESSURE AT CARB AIR TEMP A	B	C	D	FUEL FLOW LB/HR	RATED POWER (%)
1950	S.L. 5,000 10,000 14,000	28.2 27.2 26.1 25.8	29.1 27.9 26.8 25.8	29.3 28.3 27.2	30.8 31.2 28.2	664 602	52% 1300
1900	S.L. 5,000 11,000 14,500	28.3 26.9 26.0 26.0	28.7 27.8 25.8 25.7	29.2 28.4 27.4	32.3 28.7 27.0	648 582	51% 1250
1850	S.L. 5,000 12,000 14,000	27.8 26.7 25.8 24.7	28.7 27.3 25.6 25.3	28.5 27.6 27.1	29.8 28.6 27.7	626 566	49% 1225
1800	S.L. 5,000 10,000 12,500	27.8 26.7 25.6 24.7	28.3 27.9 26.6 25.3	28.9 27.7 26.8	27.9 28.9 27.3	636 568	48% 1200
1700	S.L. 5,000 10,000 12,500	27.2 25.6 24.5 23.6	27.9 26.2 27.3 24.2	28.3 26.6	28.0 27.3	502 453	[illegible] 1200
1650	S.L. 5,000 11,000 12,700	27.0 25.4 24.1 23.5	27.8 25.2 24.4 24.5	28.2 26.8	28.9	487 441	38% 950
1600	S.L. 5,000 10,000 12,500	26.5 25.4 23.9 23.2	27.3 26.2 24.6 23.6	28.1 26.5	28.8	461 427	37% 925

NOTE:-

1. Altitudes shown are carburetor top deck pressure altitudes.
2. The following carburetor air temperatures apply to these columns

ALT (FT)	A	B	C	D
S.L.	59°F	80°F	79°F	101°F
5,000	12°	62°	57°	82°
10,000	5°	24°	39°	64°
15,000	23°	7°	32°	41°

3. Avoid operating in the following restricted ranges: 700–1110 rpm, 1550–1750 rpm, 2040–2310 rpm, above 2650 rpm.
4. (*) On engines operating with accessory loads, reduce BMEP settings by 2 psi.
5. "FUEL FLOW" column indicates probable range of fuel flows for particular power setting.
6. "RATED POWER" column lists percentage of the normal rated power.
7. (-----) Altitudes underlined with a dashed line represent critical carburetor top deck pressure altitudes on a standard day.

B M E P POWER SETTINGS

AUTO-LEAN CRUISE

P&W R4360-4A ENGINES

BRAKE MEAN EFFECTIVE PRESSURE (GAUGE) (*)

RPM	[illegible] BMEP ALT (FT)	MANIFOLD PRESSURE AT CARB AIR TEMP A	B	C	D	FUEL FLOW (LB/HR)	RATED POWER (%)
[illegible]	S.L. 5,000 6,260	35.1 34.1 31.8	36.2 36.2 34.8	36.7 36.5	37.6	7[illegible] 656	64% 1600
[illegible]	S.L. 5,[illegible] 2,[illegible]	35.6 34.6 33.8	36.1 35.0 34.8	38.3 38.5	37.3	7[illegible] 636	63% 1575
[illegible]	S.L. 5,000 5,600	34.8 33.9 33.4	35.3 34.9 34.4	36.4	37.3	6[illegible] [illegible]	61% 1525
[illegible]	S.L. 5,000 5,250	34.6 35.1 33.2	35.7 34.1 34.2	36.2	37.[illegible]	660 590	59% [illegible]
[illegible]	S.L. 5,300	32.2 32.2	34.2 33.2	35.7	39.[illegible]	5[illegible]	57% [illegible]
[illegible]	S.L. 3,350	35.[illegible] 32.3	36.1 35.1	34.3	35.3	5[illegible] 463	48% 1200
[illegible]	S.L. 2,400	33.2 32.1	34.2 33.4	35.5	35.4	442 450	46% 1150

RPM	[illegible] BMEP ALT (FT)	MANIFOLD PRESSURE AT CARB AIR TEMP A	B	C	D	FUEL FLOW (LB/HR)	RATED POWER (%)
[illegible]	S.L. 5,000 7,800	33.8 32.4 31.5	34.8 33.4 32.9	36.1 35.9	36.0 36.1	645 [illegible]	60% 1500
[illegible]	S.L. 5,300 7,300	33.3 32.2 32.7	34.3 33.2 32.4	34.8 33.7	35.7 34.8	563 56[illegible]	59% 1475
[illegible]	S.L. 5,300 7,100	[illegible] 33.8 33.5	[illegible] 32.8 32.5	34.6 32.3	35.8 34.7	545 5[illegible]	57% [illegible]
[illegible]	S.L. 5,200 7,100	32.8 3[illegible] 3[illegible]	35.6 32.5 32.[illegible]	34.7 33.6	35.2 35.8	624 588	56% 1400
[illegible]	S.L. 5,600 1,500	31.5 31.2 32.1	32.5 3[illegible] 31.9	33.8	39.8	5[illegible] 558	46% 1150
[illegible]	S.L. 5,000 5,100	31.4 30.1 30.1	33.4 31.8 31.8	32.9	33.7	467 442	45% 1125
[illegible]	S.L. 4,900	31.4 30.1	32.8 31.0	32.4	33.7	455 424	43% 1075

RPM	[illegible] BMEP ALT (FT)	MANIFOLD PRESSURE AT CARB AIR TEMP A	B	C	D	FUEL FLOW (LB/HR)	RATED POWER (%)
[illegible]	S.L. 5,000 7,850	31.8 32.7 29.5	32.8 31.6 30.5	33.8 32.1	34.1 32.9	445 534	56% 1400
[illegible]	S.L. 5,000 8,000	31.5 31.8 29.3	32.8 31.3 30.4	33.3 31.4	33.9 32.6	535 545	54% 1450
[illegible]	S.L. 5,000 8,322	31.4 31.2 29.3	32.4 31.1 30.2	32.8 31.1	33.7 32.5	537 508	53% 1325
[illegible]	S.L. 5,000 8,100	31.[illegible] 29.9 29.[illegible]	32.3 30.8 30.0	32.8 31.3	33.6 32.0	505 529	52% 1320
[illegible]	S.L. 5,000 7,600	29.9 28.8 27.9	30.8 29.5 28.8	31.3 29.8	32.0 30.7	475 429	43% 1075
[illegible]	S.L. 5,000 7,555	27.9 26.9 27.8	30.8 29.4 28.6	31.3 29.8	32.9 31.6	457 418	42% 1050
[illegible]	S.L. 5,000 7,600	29.9 28.4 21.9	32.8 26.3 28.8	2[illegible].3 24.7	32.0 30.5	413 398	40% 1000

RPM	[illegible] BMEP ALT (FT)	MANIFOLD PRESSURE AT CARB AIR TEMP A	B	C	D	FUEL FLOW (LB/HR)	RATED POWER (%)
[illegible]	S.L. 5,000 15,000 12,200	30.0 28.8 27.6 27.4	33.6 29.9 28.9 28.2	31.4 30.1 29.3	32.3 30.5 29.8	5[illegible] 340	52% 1300
[illegible]	S.L. 5,000 15,000 [illegible]	29.7 28.7 27.8 27.2	33.4 29.6 28.6 28.6	31.1 27.8 28.6	31.9 31.6	536 [illegible]	50% 1250
[illegible]	S.L. 5,000 10,000 11,600	29.4 28.7 27.4 27.1	31.5 29.2 28.2 27.8	31.0 27.6 28.4	31.7 31.4	544 5[illegible]	49% 1225
[illegible]	S.L. 5,000 15,000 11,452	29.4 28.1 27.1 27.0	31.5 29.5 27.1 27.4	32.8 29.4 29.3	31.5 33.2	5[illegible] 495	48% 1200
[illegible]	S.L. 5,000 16,000	28.2 28.5 28.8	29.8 27.9 26.6	29.5 29.1	31.3 28.8	444 432	44% 1100
[illegible]	S.L. 5,200 4,758	28.3 27.0 25.6	28.2 27.6 25.4	29.6 28.2	31.6 28.3	427 393	38% 950
[illegible]	S.L. 5,000 9,400	28.3 27.3 25.9	29.2 27.9 24.9	29.3 28.3	31.4 29.2	4[illegible] 374	37% 925

NOTES:

1. Altitudes shown are carburetor deck pressure altitudes.
2. The following carburetor air temperatures apply to these columns.

ALT (FT)	A	B	C	D
S.L.	30°F	65°F	79°F	100°F
5,000	12°	47°	57°	82°
10,000	-5°	28°	38°	64°
15,000	-21°	5°	22°	47°

3. Avoid operating in the following restricted ranges: [illegible] rpm, 1550-1750 rpm, [illegible] rpm, above [illegible] rpm.
4. (*) On engines operating with accessory loads, reduce BMEP settings by 2 psi.
5. "FUEL FLOW" column indicates probable range of fuel flows for particular power setting.
6. "RATED POWER" column lists percentage of the normal rated power.
7. (.....) Altitudes underlined with a dashed line represent critical carburetor top deck pressure altitudes on a standard day.

AUTO-LEAN CRUISE

AUTO-LEAN CRUISE

2-12 - DESCENT -

2-12.1 Power Reduction - Descents are to be made at cruising power unless nature of flying conditions requires a large reduction in power in which case reduce rpm as well as manifold pressure. Avoid prolonged high rpm with low manifold pressure. If manifold pressure is to be maintained below 20 in. hg, reduce rpm below 2000.

2-12.2 Carburetor Ice is formed on or near the throttle valve when it is in a partially-closed position. In this position, the throttle valve causes a restricted flowarea and creates a pressure differential across the throttle valve. This causes a reduction in temperature, which cools the throttle and surrounding areas and causes moisture to collect on them. It is usually assumed that this type of ice forms when descending through the clouds - that is, when using reduced power.

(a) If prolonged part throttle operation is required in icing atmosphere, especially in instrument weather, maintain the carburetor air temperature at 15°C by placing the Carb Air temp switches (located on the engineer's engine panel) in the HOT position as required.

(b) If ice does form before the above preventative action can be taken, it will be indicated as follows:

1. Falling off of manifold and bmep pressures.
2. Erratic operation due to ice on metering elements.
3. In some cases, by jamming of throttle.

(c) Removal of ice already formed is best accomplished by use of full carburetor heat. If the preheat capacity is sufficient and the remedial action has not been delayed, it is a matter of seconds until the ice is removed. The preheat capacity can be increased by applying more power and by closing the cowl flaps. If the ice formation is allowed to progress to a critical extent the loss of power may make it impossible to generate sufficient heat to clear the engine. Because of this possibility it is imperative that the crew be alert to possible icing conditions and take remedial action while it can still be effective. Operation of the engine at high bmep (large throttle opening and low rpm) may assist in minimizing the possibility of ice by reducing this obstruction across the airflow. Also, a change of altitude may result in finding ice-free conditions.

2-13 BEFORE LANDING -

PILOT	ENGINEER
1. Notify crew to prepare for landing.	
2. Check landing weight and center of gravity. **NOTE** Do not land with center of gravity forward of 26% MAC or aft of 34% MAC.	
	3. Transfer throttles to pilot's control.
4. Throttle Transfer switches to PILOT.	
	5. Oil Flaps AUTO.
	6. Carb Air COLD.
	7. Mixture RICH.
	8. Cowl Flaps CLOSED.
	9. Firewall Fuel Valves NORMAL.
	10. Booster pumps and Transfer Pumps ON.
	11. Emergency Pump OFF.
	(a) No. 8 emergency tank OPEN.
	12. Wing Tanks FULL.
13. Auto Pilot OFF.	
14. Auto FT (flying tab) OFF.	

PILOT	ENGINEER
15. Flaps - lower as required in increments of 10 degrees. **NOTE** Do not lower flaps above 110 mph (95.5 knots) with power ON or 122 mph (106 knots) with power OFF. 16. Props 2550 rpm.	
	17. <u>Engine Operating Limits</u> - Oil Pressure Oil Temperature Carb Air Temp Fuel Pressure Cyl Head Temp

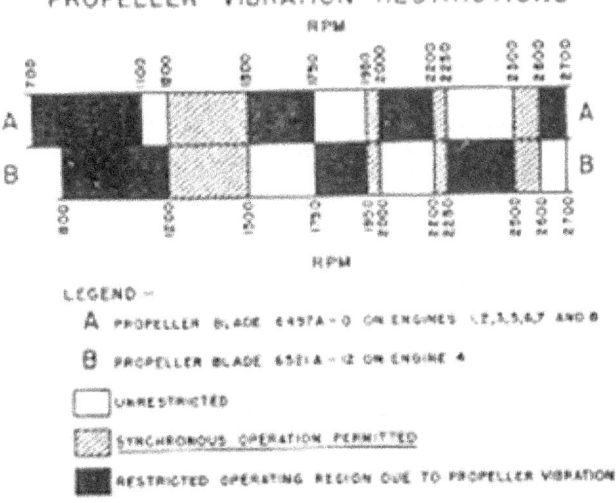

2-14 LANDING - In general, the landing stability of the airplane is good, however from the results of model tests, it is expected that light skipping may be encountered when landing at trims from 4° to 6°, but due to the deep step, the skipping will not be violent. Sufficient speed above stalling speed should be maintained to insure maneuverability, particularly under bad visibility conditions. Avoid contacting the tip floats with water during landing while above hump speed, 58-64 mph (50-55 knots).

CAUTION

IN ORDER TO MAINTAIN HYDRAULIC PRESSURE, ENGINE SPEEDS MUST BE ABOVE 1150 RPM.

2-14.1 Landing Emergencies - For landing emergencies refer to Chapter 3-6.

2-14.2 Performance Characteristics - For performance characteristics refer to Chapter 6-7.

2-15 AFTER LANDING -

PILOT	ENGINEER
	1. Cowl Flaps OPEN.
	2. Booster pumps OFF.
	3. Engine Generator Power OFF. (Eng 1, 3, and 7)
	NOTE Continuous operation for periods of more than 15 minutes duration with the generators inoperative will result in discharging the storage batteries unless the APUs are operating and carrying the electrical load.
4. Flaps UP.	
NOTE When taxiing on the step a trim angle of 4° should be maintained.	
	5. Engine Operating Limits - RPM 2550, BMEP 178, Cyl Head Temp 232°C

PILOT	ENGINEER
	6. Bilge Water Check - The bilges will be checked for water after each fast taxi run and each landing. One crew member will enter the bilge compartments and make a visual inspection for the presence of any water. **WARNING** BE SURE TO USE A SAFETY TYPE FLASHLIGHT FOR ALL WORK BELOW THE CARGO DECK FLOOR. BE SURE TO CLOSE ALL DOORS AFTER LEAVING EACH COMPARTMENT.
7. Have crew stand by for mooring.	

2-16 MOORING AND ANCHORING -

2-16.1 Mooring Procedure -

(a) Three crew members will man stations on the forward cargo deck as follows:

1. One man at port forward cargo deck access door.
2. One man in the nose of the hull close to the bow pendant line retaining hook.
3. One man at the port forward cargo deck access door interphone station.

NOTE

The man at the interphone station will call the pilot when all three crew members are at their respective stations.

(b) Three crew members will man stations at the aft cargo deck doors as follows:

1. One man at port aft cargo deck access door.
2. One man at starboard aft cargo deck access door.
3. One man at port aft cargo deck access door interphone station.

NOTE

The man at the interphone station will call the pilot when all three crew members are at their respective stations.

(c) The airplane shall approach the mooring buoy from the leeward side with its nose as close to the direction of wind as possible. Forward speed shall be kept as low as possible with not more than four symmetrically located engines operating. Engine idling speed approximately 500 rpm. The buoy mooring line, attached to the mooring buoy, will be floating out in the direction of water current flow.

(d) The airplane will approach the mooring buoy so as to bring the floating end of the mooring line as close to the port forward cargo deck access door as possible.

NOTE

When the wind velocity is at zero mph, the buoy mooring line will trail away from the mooring buoy in the direction of the current flow. Approach to the mooring buoy under zero wind velocity conditions will be made from the trailing end of the mooring line.

(e) The pilot should attempt to stabilize the airplane water speed by the time the airplane is 600 yards from the mooring buoy. If the airplane water speed is over 2-1/2 knots and under 5-1/2 knots, the two aft sea anchors may be used.

(f) Maintain constant communication with the pilot.

(g) When the airplane has approached within 600 yards of the mooring buoy the pilot will advise the crew members stationed at the aft cargo deck access doors whether or not he wishes to use sea anchors. To the crew at the port forward access door he will order "prepare to moor".

(h) If the pilot orders "use sea anchors", the three man crew at the aft cargo deck access doors will proceed as follows:

1. Open both rear cargo deck access doors.

2. Secure doors in open position with door struts.

3. Push both aft snubbing posts to the extended position. Check engagement of spring loaded locating pin.

4. Remove sea anchors and rope from their strap tie downs.

5. Men at both aft cargo deck doors should work together.

6. On the tow line, approximately 25' from the sea anchor, take two turns around the snubbing post. Keep turns close to the airplane hull. Arrange sea anchor and a 25' coil of tow line in hands ready to throw in water.

7. Throw sea anchor and 25' of tow line into water.

8. Immediately reach down and grab the trip line. Hold trip line short, approximately 20', so that sea anchor will not fill.

9. Take one turn around snubbing post with the trip line at the outboard end of the snubbing post.

10. When advised by pilot that he wishes to use sea anchors, the men at both doors will pay out the trip line and allow the sea anchors to fill. Pay out only enough trip line to fill sea anchors.

11. Anchors may be dumped, if required, by holding the trip line and paying out on the tow line.

12. Sea anchors may be retrieved by dumping and hauling in with the trip line.

13. Flush sea anchors with fresh water and dry after using. Use a small boat for flushing and drying. Do not pull wet sea anchor into airplane.

NOTE

Maximum taxi speed for tieing airplane to mooring buoy is 2-1/2 knots and for filling sea anchors 5-1/2 knots. With four engines operating at an idling speed of 500 rpm and a zero mph wind, it will take:

215 yds to reduce speed from 5-1/2 knots to 2-1/2 knots.
190 yds to reduce speed from 4-3/4 knots to 2-1/2 knots.
170 yds to reduce speed from 4 knots to 2-1/2 knots.
150 yds to reduce speed from 4 knots to 2-1/2 knots.

(i) When the pilot orders "prepare to moor" the three man crew on the forward cargo deck will proceed as follows:

1. Loosen the wing nut that secures the hook holding up the eye at the free end of the bow pendant line.

2. Lift the eye off the hook and allow the weight of the bow pendant line to pull the eye down, slacking off on the 1/4" manila rope. Open the port forward cargo deck access door and secure in the forward position.

3. Remove the vise-grip pliers that secure the lizard line and allow a few feet of line to run out through the lizard pipe.

4. Reach forward and pull the lizard line through the port cargo deck access door.

5. Continue paying out on the manila rope and pulling in on the lizard line until the eye at the end of the bow pendant line can be reached by hand.

6. Connect the 1" shackle and hook to the bow pendant line eye.

7. The forward cargo deck interphone operator will then notify the pilot that the forward cargo deck crew is ready to moor.

(j) The forward cargo deck crew will now take new positions:

1. One crew member will stand in the port forward cargo deck access door entrance with a grappling hook and line ready to throw.

2. The second crew member will stand by with a grappling hook and line ready to throw in case the first man should cast and miss.

NOTE

Be sure and secure the end of each grappling hook line so that they will not be lost overboard when thrown.

(k) When the airplane has approached to within 5 feet of the buoy mooring line, cast the grappling hook so as to engage the mooring line.

(l) If the first cast should miss, do not attempt to retrieve the hook and recast it, but step aside and allow the second crew member to cast the second grappling hook. While the second hook is being cast, retrieve the first hook and prepare it for throwing.

(m) As soon as the grappling hook has engaged the mooring line, pull the mooring line in, snap the bow pendant line hook through the mooring line shackle and drop both lines into the water.

(n) Notify the pilot immediately, as soon as the mooring line and bow pendant line hit the water.

(o) Pilot will immediately stop the engines.

2-16.2 Anchoring Procedure -

(a) Dropping Anchor -

1. The pilot will select the anchorage and order the anchor to be dropped.

2. Two crew members will proceed to the port forward cargo deck access door.

16. Lower the anchor until the anchor shackle is at a convenient working height.

NOTE

To lower the anchor turn the crank handle in the lifting direction with one hand while simultaneously applying pressure to the winch ratchet release lever with the left hand. As soon as the lever moves out of the locked position, slowly turn the crank handle in the lowering direction.

17. Reach down to the hawse pipe and secure the end of the anchor cable.

18. Release the winch brake and pull enough cable off the reel to reach up to the anchor shackle.

19. Shackle the anchor cable to the anchor.

20. Lower the anchor with the davit winch and take up slack in the anchor cable until the anchor is hanging on the anchor cable with the shackle a few inches below the chine angle.

21. Slack off on the davit winch cable and reach down and lift the davit lifting hook off the anchor shackle.

22. Raise the davit winch cable to the full up position and swing the davit inboard and stow it.

23. Release the winch brake and drop the anchor.

NOTE

Pay out sufficient line to insure that the anchor will hold. In general, seven times the depth will give the maximum holding power on the anchor.

24. Lean out through the access door and grasp the anchor cable.

25. Lift a bight of slack cable up through the access door.

3. Establish interphone connection between the pilot's station and the port forward cargo deck access door station.

4. 120V power system must be ON.

5. Remove the vise-grip pliers from the lizard line.

6. Loosen the wing nut that secures the hook holding up the eye at the free end of the bow pendant line.

7. Lift the eye off the hook and allow the weight of the bow pendant line to pull the eye down, slacking off on the 1/4" manila rope a little at a time.

8. Open the port forward cargo deck access door and secure in the forward position.

9. Reach under the access door and secure hold of the lizard line.

10. Pull in on the lizard line until the end of the pendant line can be reached and pulled in through the access door.

11. Remove the anchor cable grab from its stowed position and shackle it to the end of the bow pendant line.

12. Unlock the Dzus fasteners that secure the inboard ends of the two lower anchor stowage brackets and rotate the brackets so that the anchor can be lifted straight up.

PLACE A FIRM GRIP ON THE ANCHOR FLUKES BEFORE REMOVING THE TOP STOWAGE BRACKET AND RETAIN THIS GRIP UNTIL THE ANCHOR IS SWUNG CLEAR OF THE AIRPLANE STRUCTURE.

13. Unlock the Dzus fastener that secures the forward end of the top anchor stowage bracket.

14. Turn the crank handle on the davit winch and lift the anchor clear of its stowed position.

15. Swing the davit forward and out through the access door. Be sure that the anchor is high enough to clear the door sill.

26. Attach the anchor cable grab to the anchor cable and allow the anchor cable and pendant line to slide into the water.

27. Be sure that there is sufficient slack in the anchor cable between the reel and the pendant line and that the anchor is holding before leaving the station.

28. Signal pilot that the anchor is secure.

29. Close the access door.

(b) Hoisting Anchor -

1. The pilot will order the anchor hoisted.

2. Two crew members will proceed to the port forward cargo deck access door.

3. Establish interphone connection between the pilot's station and the port forward cargo deck access door station.

4. 120V power system must be ON.

5. Open port forward cargo deck access door.

6. Start engines and taxi airplane over the anchor so as to break it free.

7. Move the anchor hoist switch to the UP position and heave in on the anchor cable.

8. Maintain close surveillance of the anchor cable and be prepared to move the anchor hoist switch to the OFF position as soon as the anchor cable grab reaches a point just below the chine angle.

9. Remove the anchor cable grab from the anchor cable and lift it and the end of the pendant line into the airplane.

10. Move the anchor hoist switch to the UP position and continue heaving in.

11. When the anchor shackle has reached a point just below the chine angle, move the anchor hoist switch to the OFF position, swing the davit out through the door, and lower the davit cable hook.

12. Signal the pilot that the anchor is up.

13. Fasten the davit cable hook to the anchor shackle.

14. Turn the davit winch and lift the anchor high enough to clear the access door sill.

CAUTION

PLACE A FIRM GRIP ON THE ANCHOR FLUKES AND RETAIN GRIP UNTIL ANCHOR IS SECURELY STOWED.

15. Swing the davit and anchor in through the access door.

16. Remove the anchor cable from the anchor.

17. Swing the anchor into the stowed position and secure the top stowage bracket with the Dzus fastener.

18. Secure the two bottom stowage brackets and push the davit into its stowage clip.

19. Heave in on the anchor cable until the end is fully retracted into the hawse pipe.

CAUTION

DO NOT DAMAGE THE HULL STRUCTURE BY STRAINING THE CABLE.

20. Pull the eye on the end of the pendant line into the airplane with the 1/4" diameter manila line.

21. Lift the eye over the securing hook and turn the wing nut down until the cable is snug.

CAUTION

DO NOT OVER-TIGHTEN THE WING NUT!

22. Coil and stow the 1/4" diameter manila line.

23. Pull the lizard line in through the lizard pipe until it is snug.

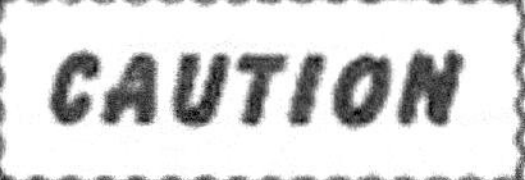

DO NOT TRY TO STRAIN THE LIZARD LINE!

24. Secure the lizard line with the vise-grip pliers and stow the slack line.

25. Signal the pilot that the anchor is stowed.

26. Close the access door.

2-17 STOPPING ENGINES -

PILOT	ENGINEER
1. Gust Locks LOCK.	
2. Throttles CLOSED.	
(a) Throttle Control switches AUTO.	
3. Direct flight engineer to stop engines.	

NOTE

Before stopping engines, cylinder head temperatures should be less than 175°C. Idle oil pressures 25 psi minimum.

PILOT	ENGINEER
	4. Mixture CUT OFF.
	5. Ignition OFF.
	6. Oil System Control Panel:
	(a) Firewall Oil Valves OPEN.
	(b) Oil Transfer OFF.
	7. Fuel System Control Panel:
	(a) Firewall Fuel Valves CLOSED.
	(b) Booster pumps OFF.
	(c) Transfer Pumps OFF. Aux (auxiliary) power OFF.
	(d) Emergency Pump OFF. Aux (auxiliary) power OFF.
	(e) Fuel Pumps Scavenge OFF.
	(f) Fuel tank valves CLOSED.
	8. Oil Flaps CLOSED.
	9. Cowl Flaps CLOSED.

NOTE

Leave cowl flaps and oil cooler flaps open for approximately 15 minutes after stopping engines.

2-18 BEFORE LEAVING AIRPLANE -

PILOT	ENGINEER
	1. Prepare flight report.
2. Pilot's pedestal flight controls in following position: (a) Gust Locks LOCK. **CAUTION** THE AILERON, RUDDER, AND ELEVATOR SHUTOFF VALVES MUST BE "ON" WHEN THE HYDRAULIC GUST LOCKS ARE LEFT IN THE LOCKED POSITION FOR MORE THAN AN HOUR AT A TIME. (b) Aux Hyd Pumps OFF. (c) Master Cyl Valves OFF. (d) Flaps UP. (e) Trim Tab Master switches OFF. (f) Radio OFF. (g) Auto Pilot and Auto FT (flying tab) power OFF.	
3. Cage gyros.	
	4. Aux Hyd Sys Master Switches OFF.
	5. Battery control. (a) 120V batteries L and R OFF. (b) 24V (28V DC) battery switch OFF.
	6. APU 1 and APU 2 OFF.
	7. Dynamotors OFF.

PILOT	ENGINEER
	8. 26V inverters OFF.
	9. Auto Pilot and Auto FT (flying tab) inverters OFF.
	10. Pneumatic System switches, Sys 1 and Sys 2 OFF.
	11. Fuel and Float Comp Blower Control Panel:
	(a) Fuel and Float Comp Blowers to DC.
	(b) Float Comp Blowers STANDBY.
	(c) Fuel Comp Vent Blower STANDBY.

FUEL AND FLOAT COMPARTMENT BLOWER CONTROL PANEL

TABLE OF CONTENTS

SECTION III - EMERGENCY OPERATING INSTRUCTIONS

TABLE OF CONTENTS

SECTION III - EMERGENCY OPERATING INSTRUCTIONS

3-1 ENGINE FAILURE -

3-1.1 Procedure on Encountering Engine Failure -

(a) Feathering Procedure - If the throttle is closed before the feathering push-button switch is operated, the propeller will move to a lower pitch. This increases the time required for the blades to reach the full-feathered position. If the governor control is moved to a lower governing speed before the feathering push-button switch is actuated, the blades will assume a higher angle, but at a rate somewhat slower than if the propeller were operated by the feathering pump. Again, the net time to feather the propeller will be longer. To feather the propeller in the shortest possible time operate the controls in accordance with the procedure outlined below.

1. Depress feathering button.
2. Throttle CLOSE.
3. Mixture CUT OFF.
4. Firewall Fuel Valve CLOSED.
5. Ignition OFF after propeller stops turning.
6. Generator OFF (Eng 1-3-7).
7. Fuel booster pump OFF.
8. Cowl Flaps CLOSE.

(b) Unfeathering Procedure - Caution should be taken regarding unfeathering in cases where the propeller was feathered because of a damaged engine, as returning the engine to operation may result in further damage. Under such conditions, it may prove impossible to feather the propeller again due to damage to oil passages in the engine.

1. Firewall Oil Valve OPEN.
2. Governor control to minimum rpm position.
3. Crack throttle open to approximate starting position.
4. Firewall Fuel Valve ON.
5. PULL feathering button and HOLD out until engine speed is approximately 1000 rpm.
6. Ignition ON after propeller has turned at least three revolutions.
7. After fuel pressure is attained, move mixture control to AUTO RICH and adjust throttle to proper manifold pressure for engine warm up.
8. Allow engine to warm up at low rpm.

3-1.2 Engine Failure During Takeoff -

(a) Failure of an engine during takeoff may not be noticed immediately except for a slight yaw. If a yaw develops due to engine failure and there is sufficient area ahead, close the throttles and stop straight ahead.

(b) If it is necessary to continue the takeoff, even though one or more engines have failed, proceed as follows:

1. Obtain directional control by using rudder with a minimum of aileron. If necessary, the opposite engine may be throttled back to obtain directional control.
2. Pick up airspeed before attempting to climb.
3. Gradually raise flaps at safe airspeed and altitude.
4. If excessive power is being used, reduce this power as soon as possible.
5. Determine which engine has failed and feather the propeller (Paragraph 3-2.2).

3-1.3 Landing With Partial Power - To land with one or more engines inoperative the following procedure should be observed:

(a) Maintain 125 percent of stalling speed (See Stalling Speeds Chart).

(b) Throttle back opposite engine/engines thereby reducing the necessity for rudder trim.

(c) Lower flaps as required in increments of 10 degrees.

(d) Throttle back the live engines and adjust trim tabs to approximately neutral just prior to the landing flare-out. Make a normal "fast-step" landing and avoid contacting tip floats with water while above hump speed.

3-1.4 Takeoff With Partial Power - This procedure is to be used only when it is necessary to fly the airplane with one or more engines inoperative from a facility which is not equipped to make engine repairs. This procedure does not apply in the event of engine failure on takeoff, or in the event of a reduced power takeoff.

(a) Seven Engine Takeoff - If a takeoff is to be accomplished with one engine inoperative, the procedure to be followed would be to throttle back the engine symmetrically located to the inoperative engine and make a takeoff using the remaining six engines.

(b) Six Engine Takeoff - The most critical takeoff condition exists when engines No. 1 and No. 2 are inoperative and a six engined asymmetric takeoff is to be accomplished. Under this condition, takeoff distances are greatest and directional control most critical. Because of the increased torque created by the unbalanced thrust, the rudder must be deflected in the direction that will counteract this force. At low speeds, rudder deflection alone may not overcome the torque produced by the asymmetric power configuration; therefore, power should be reduced on the engines symmetrically located to the inoperative engines while maintaining rudder deflection. As the speed increases and the rudder becomes more effective begin to increase power on the other two good engines until their full takeoff power is established. Hold a flap setting of 20 degrees and maintain zero degrees elevator until on the step at which time it is desirable to trim for minimum resistance as soon as possible, by gradually applying 5 degrees up elevator until airborne. Level off and accelerate to a safe climbing speed (120% of stalling speed). Immediately after becoming airborne, aileron should be coordinated with rudder, and trim applied as required. Flaps should gradually be raised at a safe altitude and airspeed.

3-2 PROPELLER FAILURE -

3-2.1 Overspeeding - Care should be taken to distinguish between the momentary overspeeds which may occur in violent maneuvers (or if manifold pressure is increased suddenly) and true run-aways in which the propeller is uncontrollable and may reach extremely high speeds. The former are due to the time lag required for the governor to react and the propeller to change pitch. The increase in rpm over the governor setting is not large, and after a brief period, the rpm returns to the governor setting. While ordinarily a run-away propeller on a multi-engine aircraft such as the HFB should be promptly feathered, under certain critical flight conditions such as during takeoff it may be advisable to continue the propeller in operation by reducing the manifold pressure, in order to utilize all possible power.

3-2.2 Failure to Feather - If, due to damage or other causes, it is impossible to feather the propeller, an attempt should be made to windmill the propeller at the lowest possible rpm. As the windmilling rpm increases with air speed, it is desirable to fly at not more than 20 to 30 mph (17 to 26 knots) above stalling speed. The controls on the windmilling engine should be placed in the following positions:

(a) Prop RPM toggle switch LOW rpm.
(b) Mixture CUT OFF.
(c) Ignition OFF.
(d) Throttle CLOSE.
(e) Firewall Fuel Valve CLOSED.
(f) Generator OFF (Eng 1-3-7).

3-2.3 Emergency Feathering Procedure -

(a) Depress feathering button.
(b) Throttle CLOSE.
(c) Mixture CUT OFF.
(d) Firewall Fuel Valve CLOSED.
(e) Ignition OFF after propeller stops turning.
(f) Generator OFF on engine feathered (Eng 1-3-7).
(g) Fuel booster pump OFF.
(h) Cowl Flaps CLOSE.

3-3 FIRE AND FIRE EXTINGUISHING -

3-3.1 Engine Fire - If any of eight individual ENG (engine) fire warning lights located on flight engineer's engine panel become illuminated, use following procedure:

(a) Close throttle.
(b) Depress feathering button.
(c) Emergency switch ON.
(d) Firewall Oil Valve CLOSED after propeller stops rotating.
(e) Select 3A and 3B system bottles on proper side - ON (Flt Engr Elec Inst Panel).
(f) Raise plastic guard on ENG (engine) fire extinguisher switch, hold switch up for 3 seconds minimum (30 seconds max.).
(g) Turn ignition switch OFF.
(h) If dead engine is one of generator equipped engines (1-3-7), place generator switch at OFF.
(i) Remove personnel from area and close wing leading edge access door.

3-3.2 Nacelle and Wing Leading Edge Fire - Any of eight individual NAC (nacelle) fire warning lights becoming illuminated on the flight engineer's engine panel indicates a fire located in the wing leading edge, between the outboard engine and the wing leading edge access door. Check nacelle area concerned to determine the extent of the fire and action to be taken. If fire is so large that it can't be controlled by the portable fire extinguishers located at nacelles 2-4-5-7, then use the steps outlined below:

(a) Remove personnel from area and close wing leading edge access door.
(b) Depress feathering button.
(c) Emergency switch ON.
(d) Firewall Oil Valve CLOSED after propeller stops rotating.
(e) Select 3A and 3B system bottles on proper side - ON (Flt Engr Elec Inst Panel).
(f) Raise plastic guard on NAC (nacelle) fire extinguisher switch, hold switch up for 3 seconds minimum (30 seconds max.).
(g) Ignition OFF.
(h) Generator switch OFF
(i) After it has been determined that the fire hazard is over purge CO_2 and any fumes from the area (Paragraph 3-4.3).
(j) A fire observer equipped with a smoke mask and a portable CO_2 bottle must investigate to determine cause of fire and steps necessary to prevent a reoccurrence while in flight. Extent of damage must be determined and flight conditions regulated as required.

NOTE

Placing one of the emergency switches ON accomplishes the following:

1. Closes hydraulic system firewall shutoff valve (Eng 2-4-5-6).
2. Closes fuel system firewall shutoff valve.
3. Closes oil system firewall shutoff valve.
4. Places mixture control at CUT OFF.
5. Opens cowl flaps.
6. Opens oil cooler flaps.

3-3.3 Hull Fuel Compartment Fire - If any of seven individual hull fuel compartment Fire Warning signals located on flight engineer's electrical instrument panel become illuminated, use the following procedure:

(a) Select 3A system or 3B system bottles ON.
(b) Raise plastic guard on hull fuel compartment fire extinguisher switch, hold up for 3 seconds minimum (30 seconds max.).

NOTE

When hull fuel tank fire extinguisher system is discharged into any particular hull bay, the hull tank ventilator fan for that bay automatically turns OFF and hull tank ventilator light goes ON. Place hull tank ventilator back in operation by turning ON regular hull tank ventilator switch.

3-3.4 APU Fire - If either of two individual fire warning signals becomes illuminated, use the following procedure:

(a) Turn fuel off at APU cabinet if possible, otherwise, turn fuel off at wing tanks.
(b) Generator OFF.
(c) Ignition OFF.
(d) Select 1A system or 1B system bottle - ON.
(e) Raise plastic guard on APU fire extinguisher switch, hold switch up for 3 seconds minimum (30 seconds max.).

NOTE

When APU fire extinguisher system is discharged, APU engine cooling air intake and air exhaust ducts close automatically. They can be reopened only by cooling-air damper switches located on APU engine instrument panel.

3-3.5 Emergency Operation of Fire Extinguishing System -

(a) Emergency Fuse Jump Switches - Three guarded single-pole normal open switches are on right side of flight engineer's engine panel. When closed, they are wired into fire extinguisher fuse circuits and are able to jump or by-pass normal fire extinguisher system fuses. These switches are for use only if a fuse should blow at a critical moment and there is no time to trace through circuits for blown fuses.

(b) Safety Valves - Two Crosby, JMB-112-C, 900 psi, pressure relief valves are incorporated in the fire extinguisher system. One valve is in the hull fuel tank and APU line. One valve is in the lines leading to wing components. Both valves are connected to a common discharge line which leads overboard.

(c) Cross Feed Systems - Cross feed systems are used only when normal operation cannot function and when CO_2 supply in any particular system (right wing, left wing, etc.) has been exhausted. Three Cross Feed control switches are located directly below the grouped cylinder control switches.

1. Example of Use of Cross Feed System - During attempt to extinguish fire in engine No. 7, both right wing systems A and B have been discharged. Use the following procedure to discharge left wing system into No. 7 engine.

   a. Right wing and left wing Cross Feed switches ON.
   b. 3A and 3B system Left Wing bottle switches ON.
   c. Raise plastic guard on No. 7 engine fire extinguisher switch, hold switch up for 3 seconds minimum (30 seconds max.).

2. Example of Use of Cross Feed System - Both A and B left wing systems have now been discharged and still more CO_2 is needed for No. 7 engine. Discharge hull tank system into No. 7 engine as follows:

   a. Left Wing Cross Feed switch OFF.
   b. Right Wing Cross Feed switch ON.
   c. Hull Tank Cross Feed switch ON.
   d. 3A system and 3B system Hull Tank bottle switches ON.
   e. Raise plastic guard on No. 7 engine fire extinguisher switch, hold switch up for 3 seconds minimum (30 seconds max.).

3-3.6 Cargo Deck Fire -

(a) Use portable fire extinguishers to control fire.
(b) Remove all unnecessary personnel to flight deck.
(c) Close empennage door valve.
(d) Close aft cargo doors.
(e) Close companionway door.

3-3.7 Flight Deck Fire -

(a) Use portable fire extinguishers to control fire.
(b) Remove all unnecessary personnel to cargo deck.
(c) Close flight deck vent valve.
(d) Close wing leading edge access doors.
(e) Close companionway door.
(f) After extinguishing fire remove smoke by opening flight deck valve.

3-4 SMOKE ELIMINATION -

3-4.1 Cargo Compartment - Smoke and/or fumes may be eliminated as follows:

(a) Open aft cargo door vents.
(b) Open empennage door valve.
(c) Increase air flow to remove smoke and/or fumes.
(d) Close wing leading edge access doors if air flows from wing leading edge to flight deck.

3-4.2 Flight Deck Compartment - Smoke and/or fumes may be eliminated as follows:

(a) Open flight deck valve.
(b) Open wing leading edge access doors.
(c) Open companionway door.
(d) Increase vent air flow.
(e) Operate wing leading edge blowers as required.
(f) Close companionway door if air flows from cargo compartment to flight deck.

3-4.3 Nacelle and Wing Leading Edge - Smoke and/or fumes may be eliminated as follows:

(a) Turn on wing leading edge blowers.
(b) Open wing leading edge doors.
(c) Increase ventilation airflow.
(d) Close companionway door if pressure on flight deck is insufficient to force air out through both the wing leading edge access door and the companionway door.

3-5 BAIL OUT - The proper method of bailing out is contingent on time, altitude, and condition of airplane; time permitting, the most practical bail out exit is either aft cargo deck access door. If time does not permit moving to the cargo deck, personnel on the flight deck will use the two rear flight deck access doors as emergency exits. Personnel on the cargo deck will then use the two forward and the two aft cargo deck access doors as exits. (See Emergency Exits Diagram.)

PILOT	ENGINEER
1. Have radio operator notify the company tower as to course, altitude, position, and nature of emergency.	
2. Give order to abandon airplane over interphone. Bailout Signal ON.	

NOTE

Multiple ringing of alarm bells and flashing of emergency red lights is the signal to abandon airplane. The bells are located on the cargo deck at stations 353, 1015, and 1566, and the red lights are located in the wing at the rear of each nacelle.

PILOT	ENGINEER
	3. The second flight engineer will supervise abandoning ship on the flight deck.
	4. Crew member stationed at the aft cargo deck door will supervise abandoning ship from the cargo deck.

NOTE

Bail Out Order:

1. Passengers or observers.
2. Flight test personnel.
3. Flight mechanics.
4. Radio operator.
5. Copilot.
6. Engineers.
7. Pilot.

EMERGENCY EXITS

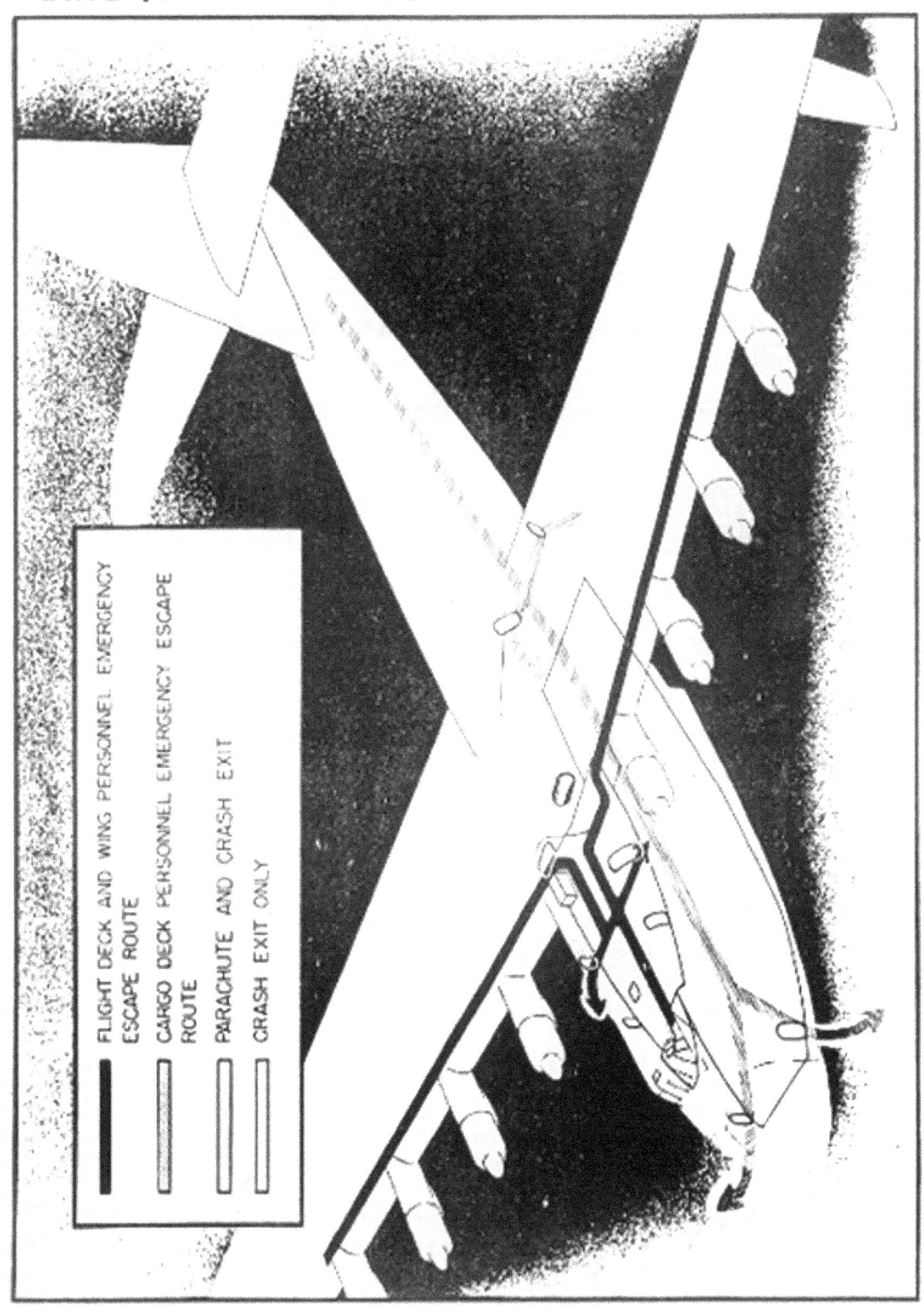

3-5.1 Use of Parachute - Every person aboard during a flight should have a parachute adjusted to fit him. Care should be taken in adjusting the harness so it will be very snug across the thighs and the shoulder straps should be adjusted to the individuals build. Adjust the parachute before flight, and either wear it or stow it in a convenient and readily accessible place.

(a) A headlong dive is the best way to leave the airplane.

(b) Grasp ripcord ring POCKET while jumping.

(c) Straighten your legs as soon as you are clear of the airplane and before you pull the ripcord.

(d) After you are sure that you are clear of the airplane, pull the ripcord all the way out on the first pull.

(e) Check oscillations as soon as possible by grasping the lines on the side of the parachute which is tending to rise, and pull them down about six inches. As the swing reverses, transfer your pull to the opposite side of the canopy.

(f) Have knees bent slightly when contact is made with the ground.

(g) Reef in lower shroud lines to deflate canopy if wind is blowing.

(h) If landing is in water, unbuckle chest and leg straps prior to contact; this supports your weight at the armpits and allows you to drop clear of the parachute and harness by raising your arms over your head. This should be done a few feet above the water so that the canopy will drift aside and not foul you in the water.

(i) DO NOT under any circumstances inflate your life jacket until you are in the water and free of your parachute.

3-5.2 Use of Life Jacket (Mae West) - The aircraft type life jacket is normally inflated by pulling the CO_2 release cords on the lower left and right sides of the jacket. The two rubber tubes on the front may be used to inflate the jacket with the mouth.

3-6 LANDING EMERGENCIES -

3-6.1 Rough Water Landings -

(a) Select a Heading -

1. Fly at 2000 feet or more and observe the direction of the swells.

2. Fly low and drag the water over several likely headings, observing surface conditions most favorable for landing.

3. Choose a heading which appears smoothest, provided it doesn't oppose the direction of swells previously observed.

4. With swell and sea in same direction and wind less than 20 knots, the best heading for landing is parallel to the crests, regardless of wind direction. Second best choice is landing down-swell. Landing into swells and wind is a poor third choice unless the wind is much faster than the swells.

(b) Select a Landing Area - Look for a relatively smooth area and try to land the airplane on the near edge.

(c) Landing -

1. Set down at minimum speed (see Stalling Speed Chart).

2. Keep wings level to the water.

3. Landings, regardless of heading, should touch down on top of a swell or within 30 to 40 feet beyond. Touching down on the face of an approaching swell should be avoided.

3-6.2 Terrestrial Landing

- If the occasion ever arises that will entail a forced landing on land, the following information may prove helpful. Due to the unpredictable circumstances that may be encountered, no definite procedure may be outlined, however, in any case the steps given below, if followed, will be found to be of value.

(a) All crew members and passengers should be immediately notified of the pilot's intentions and should cooperate fully to prepare themselves and the ship for the emergency. The wearing of life jackets is a good protective measure but may tend to hinder operations if haste is required. It is, therefore, recommended that they be put aside in a convenient location until just prior to the actual landing.

(b) The pilot's judgment will dictate the location of loose gear; if time allows, all heavy removable gear may be thrown overboard. Heavy objects, if not jettisoned, should be stowed against a bulkhead as securely as possible, to prevent their movement in event of a severe shock. Passengers should be instructed to go as far aft as possible and sit with their backs against the aft side of the bulkhead using their parachute as a back rest. Inflate life vest as extra protection for the body.

(c) All hatches should be opened and all safety belts that are to be worn shall be adjusted to fit very snugly. A loose safety belt may cause severe internal injuries in event of a severe jolt.

(d) All precautions shall be taken to prevent a possible fire hazard. Movement of fuel should be reduced to a minimum and just prior to landing the fuel transfer system should be stopped and all hull tank fuel valves should be closed. Auxiliary power units should be stopped and the fuel should be shut off at the wing tanks. All electrical power not absolutely necessary should also be turned off. Fuel fire wall valves, ignition switches, and battery switches should be turned OFF just prior to contact with the ground.

(e) Emergency disconnect at batteries should be opened just prior to contact with the ground.

3-7 AIRPLANE SYSTEMS -

3-7.1 Throttle Control System - In case normal throttle control fails, an inching control is provided. This operates through an independent system which consists primarily of a separate motor mounted on each servo unit and controlled from either pilot's or flight engineer's station by toggle switches. If both normal throttle control system and throttle inching system fail, a mechanical override system can be operated from each nacelle.

(a) Throttle Failure with Vernier OFF - If any particular engine throttle control fails to function correctly when flight engineer's vernier is OFF, proceed as follows:

1. Place the particular throttle control switch at inching.
2. Operate inching switch by momentarily toggling to desired position, OPEN or CLOSE.

(b) Throttle Failure with Vernier ON - If any particular engine throttle control fails to function correctly when Flight Eng Vernier is ON, proceed as follows:

1. Place Flight Eng Vernier at OFF.
2. Check Throttle Controls for correct operation.
3. If trouble continues, place malfunctioning Throttle Control switch at INCHING.
4. Operate Inching switch by momentarily toggling to desired position, OPEN or CLOSE.

(c) Use of Mechanical Override - If both normal throttle control system and inching system fail, and it is necessary to continue the engine in operation, use mechanical override system as follows:

1. Proceed through wing walkway to nacelle of malfunctioning control.
2. Establish interphone contact with pilot.
3. Locate emergency instruction plate for manual throttle control (inboard side).
4. Read instructions on emergency instruction plate and use them to adjust manual throttle control according to pilot's instructions.

3-7.2 Oil System - If the nacelle oil tank quantity gauge shows less than 13 gallons, and the switches are in AUTOMATIC position, it indicates possible failure of the transfer system and a quick check is to be made.

1. Check for blown fuse in indicator circuit.
2. Determine if transfer pumps are operating, if so, manually open oil transfer valves as required. If valve has failed electrically, then the oil transfer valve must be operated manually when oil is required in nacelle oil tank. The transfer switch must be in OFF position and operated manually along with the valve when oil is required.
3. Check quantity of oil in reserve tank.

3-7.3 Fuel System -

(a) Failure of Normal Fuel System - If the normal fuel system should fail or become inoperative for any reason while the airplane is in flight, the emergency fuel system operational procedure is as follows:

1. Emergency Pump ON. (Fuel pressure to outboard engines will be approximately 9 lbs/sq in.)
2. OPEN No. 8 emergency tank valve.
3. Firewall Fuel Valves in EMERGENCY position on engines affected by failure of the normal system.
4. Fuel quantity gauge selector switch to No. 8 tank.

NOTE

Before starting the takeoff run and before starting the approach for landing the Emergency Fuel System will be placed in operation, except, that the firewall fuel valves will be left in the NORMAL position. This will provide fuel under pressure as far as the firewall fuel valves and reduce the time necessary for placing the Emergency System in operation in the event of normal system failure.

(b) Transfer Pump Failure - The loss of either transfer pump during cruise flight condition calls for the following steps to be taken:

1. Defective pump switch OFF.
2. OPEN wing tank crossfeed valves manually.

(c) Emergency Operation Fuel Transfer Pumps and Emergency Fuel Pumps - If normal electrical power system fails to furnish current for operation of fuel transfer pumps and emergency fuel pumps, limited operation from storage batteries can be obtained by placing the AUX (auxiliary) switches at ON and placing either No. 1 Batt or No. 2 Batt switch ON (located at Aux Hyd Panel on cargo deck). Place Fuel Pumps Scavenge switch at AUTO. The three auxiliary power switches labeled AUX are located to left of the Regular system switches.

(d) Emergency Tanks - Hull tanks 5 and 6 are connected to the regular fuel system but are to remain empty except in case of an emergency. If a fuel tank has a leak use the following procedure to transfer the fuel to tanks 5 and 6.

1. Open valve on leaking tank and valve on empty tank 5 and allow fuel level to equalize.
2. Close valve on tank 5 and open valve on empty tank 6 and allow fuel level to equalize.
3. Close valve on tank 6 and use fuel from leaky tank to supply engines.

(e) Emergency Fuel, APUs - Emergency fuel supply for APUs is from left wing tank. A manually operated selector valve located in a recess in the lower front panel of the APU cabinet is provided for selection of normal or emergency supply systems.

(f) Hull Tank Fuel Valves Emergency (Manual) Operation - If normal operation of fuel valves is impossible because of an electrical failure, they may be operated manually. They are located under red metal covers near the centerline of the airplane on the cargo deck.

3-7.4 Electrical System -

(a) Inverter Power Switches - If normal 120V DC system fails, turn ON inverter power switches located on cargo deck auxiliary hydraulic control panel.

(b) Auxiliary Power Units (APUs) - The APUs may be used in the event the engine driven generators fail, or if the electrical loads exceed engine driven generator capacity. For starting procedure refer to Chapter 4-7.

(c) Storage Batteries - Provisions are made for connecting the main battery system in parallel to the main power bus bar to "stiffen" the electrical system and to provide emergency power for a limited period of time. Switches for controlling the battery system are located on top of the flight engineer's fuel system control panel.

3-7.5 Hydraulic Control System - To be furnished when available.

3-7.6 Pneumatic System - To be furnished when available.

3-8 FLOTATION -

3-8.1 Hull Ruptured - If the hull is ruptured permitting one to three bays forward of the CG or one or two bays aft of the CG to become flooded, the hull will float with its water line below the level of the cargo deck floor. In the case of the hull rupture forward of the CG, the maximum draught will be 8 ft and the minimum trim angle will be +1.45°. For the case of the hull rupture aft of the CG, the maximum draught will be 7.7 ft and the maximum trim angle will be 3.8°.

For more severe ruptures, the maximum water level will be at the cargo deck floor. If the hull becomes flooded in this manner, the range of positive trim angles will be between 1° and 3-1/4°. Sufficient flotation material has been added to insure longitudinal stability.

3-8.2 Loss of Tip Float, Hull Intact - In a calm sea under favorable conditions with the hull intact and the loss of one tip float, the airplane will tend to heel toward the remaining float. In a calm sea under adverse conditions the heel will be approximately 10° and the wing tip will be submerged. In a 30 mph crosswind and a corresponding sea (Beaufort No. 7) the airplane will float with a heel of approximately 20° with the wing tip submerged. Sufficient flotation material has been added to the wing tip to limit further heel.

3-8.3 Loss of Tip Float, Hull Flooded - With the loss of one tip float and the hull flooded the airplane will float at approximately the hull reference line. It will remain horizontally stable with a heel of approximately 5°

3-9 OPEN SEA OPERATION -

3-9.1 Emergency Takeoff in the Open Sea - While each situation confronted by a pilot in planning an open sea takeoff presents different aspects of wind, sea conditions, and load, successful takeoffs can be made in heavy swells and under adverse wing conditions. The following are guiding principles:

(a) Lighten the airplane by jettisoning as much removable weight as safety and balance permit.

(b) The greatest difficulty in taking off in an open sea is obtaining sufficient speed for control. Unless takeoff is being made into the wind, the run may have to be started downwind and then turned to takeoff heading.

(c) On heading parallel to crests, start on top of a crest. As the swell advances, the pilot may ease the nose of the airplane slightly down swell in an effort to keep the airplane on top of the crest throughout the run, or he may hold a course parallel to the crests. The airplane should be lifted off immediately upon reaching flying speed.

(d) If takeoff heading is down swell, accelerate the airplane gradually. Ride the nose up and down successive swells, by keeping the speed low enough to avoid leaving the water prematurely. Try to trim for best acceleration. When airplane is just below takeoff speed and is at the top of a big swell with smaller swells ahead, open throttle smartly in an effort to obtain takeoff speed and to stay in the air when the airplane reaches the top of the next swell ahead.

(e) Under complex sea conditions, study sea ahead and pick a spot where the swells appear to be in opposing phase and the surface is relatively smoother. At the moment of reaching this area, apply takeoff throttle in an effort to become airborne and to remain so when the airplane reaches the first large swell beyond the smooth spot; if possible, select a heading which will:

1. Avoid running directly into the face of any swell system.
2. Bring wind ahead as much as possible.
3. Involve a minimum of taxied turns out of the wind.

3-9.2 Use of Sea Anchors in the Open Sea - In an open sea with strong winds, the airplanes drift can be slowed and the nose kept into the wind by use of sea anchors. The sea anchors would in this case be attached to each of the forward snubbing posts.

(a) Description - One sea anchor equipped with 125 ft of 1 in. manila tow line and 100 ft of 1/2 in. manila trip line, is stowed behind each aft cargo deck access door.

(b) Use of Sea Anchors -

1. Three trained crew members will station themselves on the forward cargo deck as follows:

   a. One man at the forward cargo deck interphone station.
   b. Two men standing by for instructions.

NOTE

The man at the interphone station will call the pilot when all three crew members are on hand.

2. When the pilot orders "Use Sea Anchors", the three man crew will proceed as follows:

   a. Bring the two sea anchors from the aft to the forward cargo deck access doors.
   b. Open both forward cargo deck access doors and secure them in their forward position.
   c. Work both sea anchors at the same time.
   d. Put the sea anchors in the water. Use the trip lines for positioning the sea anchors. Keep the tow lines slack.
   e. When approximately 25 ft of trip line has been paid out secure the tow lines to the forward snubbing posts.
   f. Allow the sea anchors to fill by letting the trip lines go slack and the tow lines take the load.
   g. Coil remainder of trip and tow lines and secure them to the forward snubbing posts.
   h. Close and secure both forward cargo deck access doors.
   i. Notify the pilot that the sea anchors are dragging.

TABLE OF CONTENTS

SECTION V - OPERATING LIMITATIONS

TABLE OF CONTENTS

SECTION V - OPERATING LIMITATIONS

TABLE OF CONTENTS

SECTION V - OPERATING LIMITATIONS

5-1 MINIMUM CREW REQUIREMENTS - Crew assignment lists will be published immediately prior to flight. Additional crew members as required will be added at the discretion of the pilot. Recommended minimum crew will consist of:

(a) Pilot
(b) Copilot
(c) First Flight Engineer
(d) Second Flight Engineer
(e) Assistant Flight Engineer
(f) Radio Operator
(g) Five additional crew members to operate at the following stations:

1. One electrician to assist radio operator and maintain electrical equipment as directed by flight engineer and crew chief.

2. Two engine mechanics on flight deck to operate APU and assist in engine maintenance as directed by flight engineer and crew chief.

3. Two hydraulic mechanics located on cargo deck for operation of auxiliary hydraulic station and main hydraulic systems as directed by flight engineer and crew chief.

5-2 POWERPLANT LIMITATIONS -

5-2.1 Engine Operating Conditions -

Operating Condition	RPM	Manifold Pressure	Mixture Control	Cyl. Head Limits °C	BMEP
Takeoff Power (5 min. max.)	2550*	49.6	Auto Rich	232	202
Normal Rated Power	2550	44.3	Auto Rich	232	178
Max. Cruising Power	2230	34.0	Auto Lean	218	136
Max. Overspeed (30 seconds)	3060		Auto Rich	232	

*Restricted to 2550 rpm by propeller vibration restrictions.

5-2.2 Oil Inlet Temperature Limits -

(a) Minimum - 40°C (104°F) for all operating conditions above 800 rpm.
(b) Maximum -
- Warm up and ground tests - 85°C (185°F)
- Cruising - 85°C (185°F)
- Takeoff and rated power - 98°C (210°F)

5-2.3 Oil Pressure Limits -

(a) Minimum -
- 80 psi above 2000 rpm
- 65 psi between 1600 and 2000 rpm
- 50 psi between 1200 and 1600 rpm
- 25 psi at idle rpm

(b) Maximum - 100 psi above 1600 rpm at oil temp above 40°C.

5-2.4 Fuel Pressure Limits -

(a) Minimum -
- 14 psi at idle rpm*
- 24 psi all other operating conditions

(b) Maximum - 26 psi for all operating conditions.

5-2.5 Engine Run-Up Restrictions - Moored Airplane -

(a) During any engine operation when the airplane is in the hangar, all hangar doors immediately forward and aft of the propeller locations must be open.

(b) Not more than two engines (any combination and any power setting may be run simultaneously while the airplane is on the cradle and tied down.

(c) When the airplane is afloat in the channel immediately ahead of the jetty fingers and restrained by mooring lines, all eight engines shall not be operated simultaneously above idling rpm. If it becomes necessary to operate above idling, any two symmetrically located engines may be operated at powers up to 2000 rpm and 120 bmep maximum, at which time two other symmetrically located engines may be operated at idle rpm.

5-2.6 Propeller Vibration Restrictions -

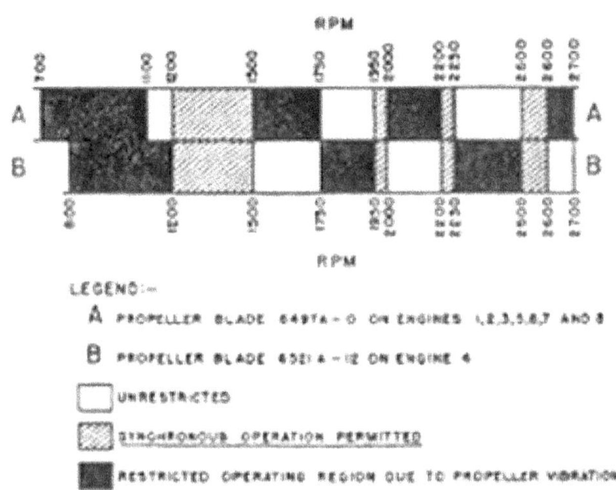

5-3 FUEL SYSTEM LIMITATIONS -

(a) The two wing tanks are to be filled (300 gals.) before starting engines. The maximum filling level for hull tanks that are to be filled is 900 gallons, as indicated on the hull fuel tank calibration chart below.

NOTE

Hull Tanks 5 and 6 are for standby purposes and are not to be filled. Hull Tanks 1, 2, 3, 4, 9, and 10 are not installed.

(b) Fuel consumption sequence is subject to the approval of the weight control engineer.

(c) Since hull tanks are at different elevations, no more than one tank should be opened to each tank manifold and the cross-feed between manifolds should be closed at all times during normal operation.

(d) Hull tank No. 8 should always be filled regardless of the total fuel load. The fuel in hull tank No. 8 should always be held in reserve and consumed last.

(e) Continued ventilation of all fuel tank compartments is required at all times. The external ventilator system should be employed if the airplane is to be docked for any appreciable length of time.

5-4 ELECTRICAL SYSTEM LIMITATIONS -

5-4.1 Starters - Starter operation is limited as follows:

(a) Open inching switch for 30 seconds to clear cylinders of any fluid.

(b) Place starter switch at START position for 60 seconds.

(c) Allow to cool for 60 seconds, followed by not more than six cycles as follows:

1. START 30 seconds.
2. Cool for 60 seconds.

(d) If it is necessary to recrank again after six attempts to start, a 30 minute cooling period is mandatory.

5-4.2 Landing Lights - Maximum operating time for ground operation, when the airplane is not in motion, is 3 minutes continuous.

5-4.3 Anchor Winch - A minimum load of not less than 20 pounds must be maintained on the anchor cable whenever the anchor winch is released. This is necessary in order to avoid fouling the anchor cable.

5-4.4 120 Volt Battery System - At maximum continuous load of 200 amps (approx), operating time is 20 minutes.

5-4.5 Edison Fire Detectors - Maximum time in TEST position is 3 seconds.

5-4.6 Fire Extinguisher Solenoids - Maximum time in ON position is 30 seconds.

5-5 HYDRODYNAMIC AND FLIGHT LIMITATIONS -

5-5.1 Hydrodynamic Limitations - It has been estimated that a fully submerged tip float will pull off at speeds above 35 mph (30.4 knots). It is important, therefore, for the pilot to keep wings level at all times during takeoff and landing.

5-5.2 Flutter and Vibration Limitations - Do not exceed 120 - 130 mph (104 - 113 knots), until the wing, tail, and control surfaces are checked for possible flutter. Rapid, continuous oscillatory motions of the controls are to be avoided, due to the possibility of exciting natural vibration modes of the airplane.

5-5.3 Speed Limitations -

(a) Maximum Glide or Dive Speed - 185 mph (161 knots) TIAS.
(b) Maximum Level Flight Speed - 185 mph (161 knots) TIAS (CG 26% to 34% MAC).
(c) Maximum Speed, Flaps Extended 45° - 122 mph (106 knots) TIAS (power OFF).

5-5.4 Stalling Speeds - Estimated stalling speeds for the power-off condition are shown below. Power-on stall information will be furnished when available.

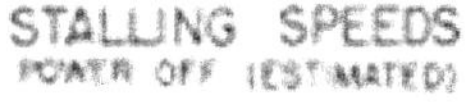

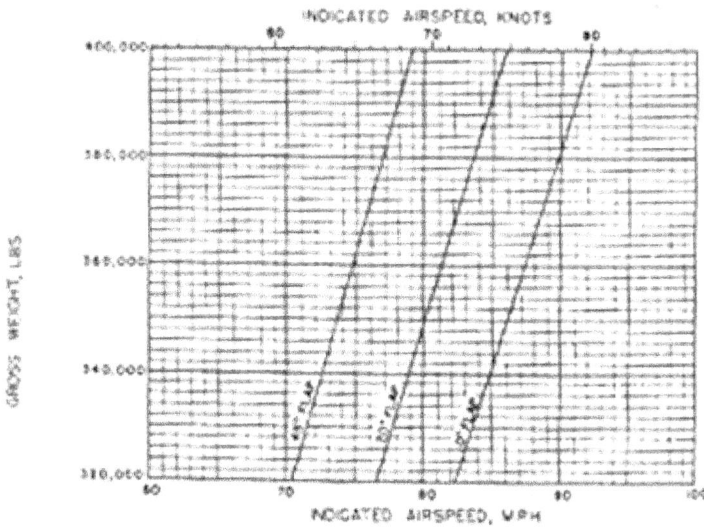

5-5.5 Prohibited Maneuvers - Spins and acrobatics are prohibited.

5-5.6 CAA Restrictions - The operation of this airplane is restricted by the CAA to visual day contact flights over territorial waters of the United States off the coast of the State of California. Occupancy of the airplane is limited to personnel essential to conduct experimental flight tests. No flight is to be conducted for hire or reward.

5-6 FLIGHT CONTROLS LIMITATIONS -

(a) Do not use aileron flying tab control system until released for operation.

(b) Always trim surfaces to zero hinge moment or zero stick force when practical during level flight.

(c) During normal hydraulic operation elevator trim tabs are to be set at 0° before maneuvering.

(d) Do not exceed 3° down aileron at 185 mph TIAS.

(e) For restrictions to be observed during changeover from hydraulic flight controls to flying tab controls, and vice versa, see Chapter 7-6 (also see (a) above).

(f) No load should be applied to the controls during operation of changeover jack-screws on hydraulic and flying tab controls (see (a) above).

(g) Cylinder by-pass valves must be open when operating on flying tab control (see (a) above).

(h) When by-passed use regular by-pass system, open alternate by-pass master valves.

(i) Always return hydraulic changeover override valve to neutral position after use.

(j) The co-pilot is responsible for maintenance of hydraulic pressure on the main and alternate hand pump systems whenever the airplane is being operated.

(k) Both gust lock levers must be unlocked before takeoff and must not be locked during flight.

(l) Check the individual system switches or levers on the pedestal for proper position before turning on any master switches or levers.

(m) Do not exceed red line on aileron position indicator whenever the flying tab system is in operation (see (a) above).

(n) Avoid abrupt movements of the controls and avoid hitting the stops violently at extremes of travel.

(o) Trim tab deflections are limited to ±13°.

5-7 WEIGHT AND BALANCE LIMITATIONS -

5-7.1 Center of Gravity Limitations - 26% MAC to 34% MAC. (See Speed Limitations Chart.)

NOTE

Recommended 28% MAC to 32% MAC for first flights.

5-7.2 Weight Limitations -

(a) Maximum gross weight for landing and takeoff - 400,000 lbs.

(b) In case of an emergency the minimum weight obtainable by jettisoning all unnecessary equipment is 284,000 lbs (hull fuel tanks empty, wing fuel tanks and hull oil tank full).

(c) Prior to each flight, all items affecting the weight and balance of the airplane, such as fuel loading, passenger and crew arrangements, and installation weight changes shall be approved by the weight control engineer.

5-8 <u>AREA RESTRICTIONS</u> - There should be no personnel in tail, wings or bilge of airplane during takeoff or landing.

5-8.1 <u>Topside Skin Walkway Areas</u> -

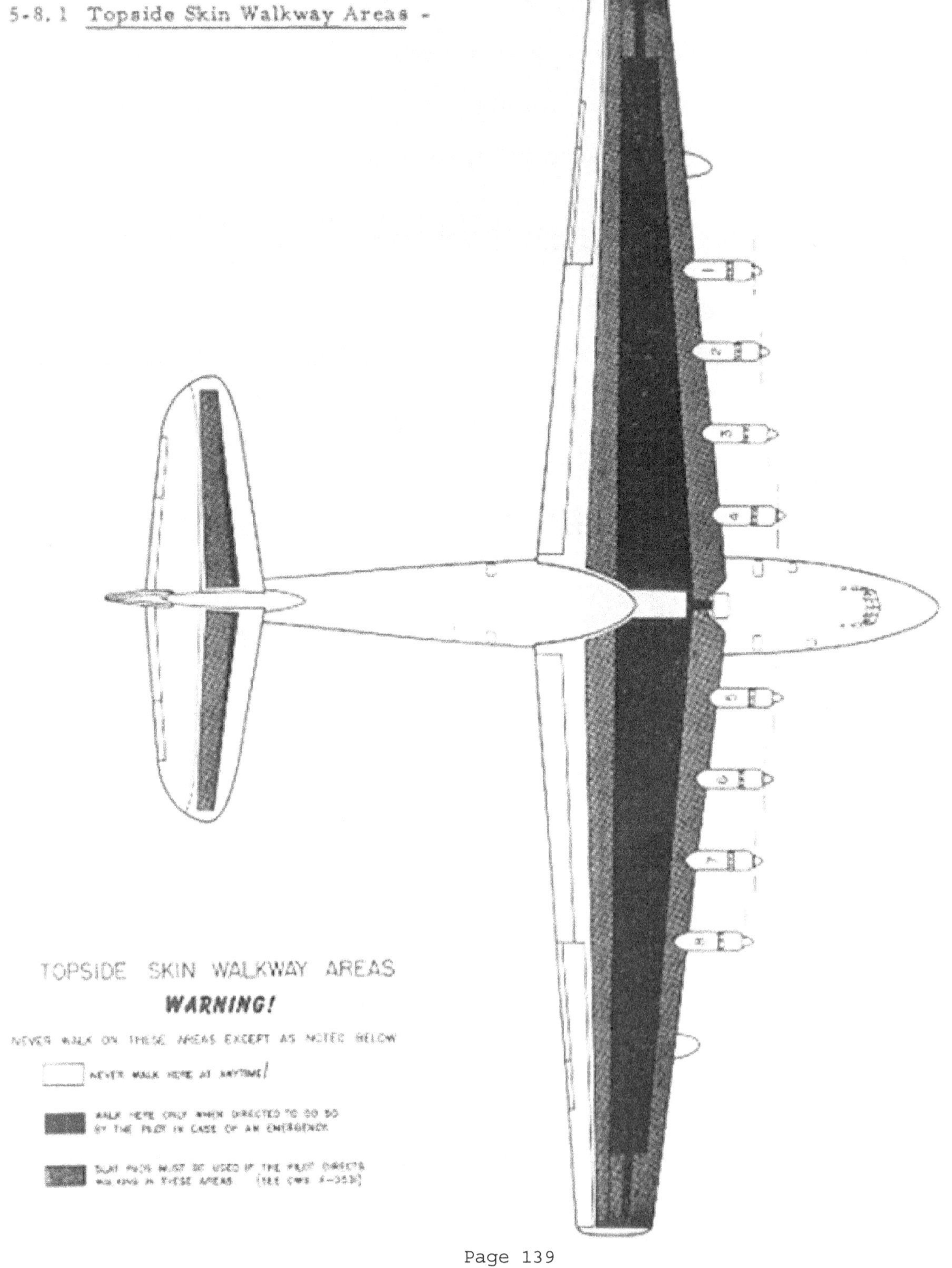
TOPSIDE SKIN WALKWAY AREAS
WARNING!
NEVER WALK ON THESE AREAS EXCEPT AS NOTED BELOW
NEVER WALK HERE AT ANYTIME!
WALK HERE ONLY WHEN DIRECTED TO DO SO BY THE PILOT IN CASE OF AN EMERGENCY
SLAT PADS MUST BE USED IF THE PILOT DIRECTS WALKING IN THESE AREAS

5-9 STRUCTURAL LIMITATIONS -

5-9.1 Normal Flight Configuration -

(a) Wing leading edge access door at station 1122 to be closed at all times.

(b) Wing rib intermediate fire curtains to be left unzipped at all times.

(c) Nacelle fire curtains to be closed at all times.

5-9.2 Wing Leading Edge or Engine Nacelle Damage - In case ram pressure is introduced into leading edge of wing:

(a) Maximum airplane velocity - 180 mph.

(b) Close wing leading edge access doors to prevent build up of pressure in the hull.

5-9.3 Flight Deck Loading is limited to:

(a) Static condition - Forty people whether in concentrated groups or individually scattered locations.

(b) Taxi condition - All seats occupied, plus 12 additional people in concentrated groups or at individually scattered locations on the flight deck.

5-9.4 Cargo Deck Loading -

(a) Cargo deck floor - Floor is designed for an equally distributed dead weight load of 122 pounds per square foot. A load factor of n = 5.0 (down) can be applied to this load.

(b) Cargo deck equipment platforms -

1. 2000 pounds concentrated dead weight load applied at center of all beams running fore and aft.
2. 4000 pounds equally distributed dead weight load applied to all beams running fore and aft for individually loaded platforms.
3. 2000 pounds equally distributed weight load applied to all beams running fore and aft when adjacent platforms are also loaded.
4. 2000 pounds equally distributed dead weight load on each frame attachment.

5-9.5 Cargo to Flight Deck Companionway -

(a) Static condition -

1. Six men on circular stairway (one man every other step).
2. Three men on walkway at foot of circular stairway.
3. Four men on straight stairway (one man every other step).

(b) Flight or landing condition -

1. Three men on circular stairway.
2. Three men on walkway.
3. Two men on straight stairway.

5-9.6 Flight Deck Extension Ladder - Designed for two men only.

5-9.7 Engine Service Platforms - Maximum of two men and 100 lbs of tools per side on designated walk areas.

5-9.8 Anchor Winch -

(a) Stalls at 1200 pound load.

(b) Slips at 1500 pound load.

5-9.9 Mooring and Snubbing Fittings -

(a) Bow fitting (Sta. 230) - 35,000 pounds horizontal to 90° down, 30° right or left.

(b) Aft warm-up or towing fitting - 35,400 pounds horizontal to 15° down, 30° right or left.

(c) Float strut warm-up fitting - to be used only while airplane is in hangar.

(d) Forward snubbing post (Sta. 192) - 9000 pounds any direction.

(e) Aft snubbing post (Sta. 1304) - 9000 pounds any direction.

(f) Tip float fitting - 2660 pounds any direction.

(g) Anchor davit - 160 pound anchor.

5-9.10 Aft Hull Walkway -

(a) Flight - One man between frames.

(b) Static - Two men between frames.

5-9.11 Wing Walkways - Interior -

(a) Flight - One man per section.

(b) Static - Two men per section.

5-9.12 Ladders in Vertical Stabilizer -

(a) Flight - One man.

(b) Static - Two men.

5-9.13 Rear Spar Platform -

(a) Flight - Two men.

(b) Static - Six men.

5-9.14 Vertical Stabilizer Rib Station 51-1/2 -

(a) Flight or taxi - One man.

(b) Static - Two men.

5-9.15 Nacelle -

(a) Flight or taxi - One man forward, one man aft.

(b) Static - Weight of four men equally distributed.

5-9.16 Tail Cone -

(a) Flight or taxi - Do not load under these conditions.

(b) Static condition - Weight of two men equally distributed over four frames with use of canvas and slat pad.

7-6.8 Flight Control Operational Check - The checks as outlined in (a), (b), and (c) below are to be accomplished by the pilot in Chapter 2-5, step No. 2.

BEFORE OPERATING THE CONTROL SYSTEM, CHECK TO INSURE THAT ALL PERSONNEL ARE CLEAR OF ALL MECHANISMS AND LINKAGES THROUGHOUT THE AIRPLANE.

(a) Main Hydraulic System Check -

PILOT	ENGINEER
1. Neutralize pilot's and copilot's controls by bringing to a position midway between extremes of valve travel.	
	2. OPEN hand pump system charging valves at hand pump reservoir.
3. Sys 1 Hydraulic Changeover lever forward (MAIN).	
a. Sys 1 Main pressure 2000 ± 50 psi.	
b. Sys 2 Main pressure 150 psi max.	
c. Sys 1 and Sys 2 Aux pressure 50 psi max.	
4. Gust Locks UNLOCK - All controls should be inoperative.	
5. Flap Hydraulics switch to Sys 1; Sys 2 OFF. Flaps should operate.	
6. Sys 1 Hyd Shutoff Valve Master switch ON and Sys 1 Ail. Hyd Shutoff valve switches OFF. Aileron should become inoperative; if so, move switch to METERED. It should be possible to move slowly; if so, move switch back to ON and aileron should again operate normally.	

PILOT	ENGINEER
7. Repeat above check for Sys 1 Rudder.	
8. Repeat above check for Sys 1 Elevator.	
9. Sys 1 Hyd Shutoff valve master switch OFF.	
10. Sys 2 Hydraulic Changeover lever forward (MAIN).	
a. Sys 1 and Sys 2 Main pressure 2000 ± 50 psi.	
b. Sys 1 and Sys 2 Aux pressure 50 psi max.	
11. Sys 1 Hydraulic Changeover lever in midposition (BY-PASS). Use Hyd Changeover Override switch to position Changeover Lever.	
a. Sys 1 Main pressure 150 psi max.	
b. Sys 2 Main pressure 2000 ± 50 psi.	
c. Sys 1 and Sys 2 Aux pressure 50 psi max.	
NOTE	
When the changeover override is used, the override lever should always be returned to neutral after changeover has been moved to the desired position.	
12. Flap Hydraulics switch to Sys 2; Sys 1 OFF. Flaps should operate.	
13. Sys 2 Hyd Shutoff Valve Master switch ON.	

PILOT	ENGINEER
14. Sys 2 Ail. Hyd Shutoff valve switch METERED. It should be possible to move aileron slowly; if so, move switch to ON and aileron should operate normally.	
15. Repeat above check for rudder.	
16. Repeat above check for elevator.	
(b) Auxiliary Hydraulic System Check -	
1. Leave Hydraulic Changeover levers as they are and start Sys 1 Aux Hyd Pump. Allow pump to attain normal operating speed.	
2. Sys 1 Hydraulic Changeover lever aft (Aux).	
a. Sys 1 Aux pressure 2000 ± 50 psi.	
b. Sys 1 Main pressure 150 psi max.	
3. Return Sys 1 Hydraulic Changeover lever to forward position (MAIN) by use of Hyd Changeover Override switch.	
4. Sys 1 Aux Hyd Pump OFF.	
5. Repeat above checks for Sys 2 Aux using the Hyd Changeover Override switch to position the Hydraulic Changeover lever.	
6. Sys 1 and Sys 2 Hydraulic Changeover levers MAIN.	
7. Operate Sys 1 Regular Cyl Valves as follows:	
a. Mast (master) ON.	

PILOT	ENGINEER

b. Ail (aileron) BY-PASS. Operate aileron to check operation of cyl by-pass valve. If open, Sys 1 pressure will fall below Sys 2 pressure while ailerons are in motion. Return Ail. Cyl Valve control to NORMAL.

c. Repeat above check on Rud (rudder).

d. Repeat above check on Elev (elevator).

e. Mast (master) OFF.

8. Repeat above check for Sys 2.

CHECK DIRECTION OF THE CONTROL SURFACE TRAVEL RELATIVE TO MOVEMENT OF THE COCKPIT CONTROLS TO INSURE THAT THEY MOVE IN THE PROPER DIRECTION.

(c) Auto-Pilot Check -

1. Controller selector AUTO-PILOT.

2. Auto Pilot Inverter LARGE, Power ON, Gyro IN, and Clutch Master ON.

3. Auto Pilot artificial horizon UNCAGED.

4. Individual servo clutches ENG, operate controller to check operation of surfaces.

5. At completion of check return all clutch switches and auto pilot switch to OFF.

6. Inverter SMALL.

(d) Flying Tab System Check - This check is to be accomplished by the pilot in Chapter 2-3, step No. 1 (b).

PILOT	ENGINEER
1. Aileron Flying Tab Check -	
a. Master changeover switch ON.	
b. Master Hyd Shutoff Valves Sys 1 and Sys 2 ON.	
c. Sys 1 and Sys 2 Ail. (aileron) Hyd Shutoff Valves OFF.	
d. Hyd Controls A and B, Ail. OFF.	
e. Ail. FT Control ENG.	
f. Ail. FT - ENG.	
g. Check operation of aileron FT by moving control wheel through full travel. An outside observer should observe action of tabs during this check. If there is any evidence of binding, insufficient travel, or other malfunctioning, the cause should be found and corrected before flight.	
h. Controller selector AUTO FT.	
i. Auto FT Inverter LARGE, Power ON, and Gyro IN.	
j. FT gyro horizon UNCAGED.	
k. Clutch Master ON.	
l. Aileron clutch ENG.	
m. Operate controller and check for proper operation of flying tab. Since the control cables are engaged to the flying tab with the aileron FT control switch in the ENGAGED position, the control wheel will follow the movement of the tab and serve as an indicator during this check. Repeat check with Gyro horizon caged and Gyro OUT.	
n. Ail. FT - OFF.	
o. Ail. FT Control OFF.	
p. Hyd Control A - Ail. ENG.	
q. Hyd Control B - Ail. OFF.	
r. Hyd Shutoff Valves, Sys 1 and 2 METERED, then ON.	

PILOT	ENGINEER
2. Rudder Flying Tab Check - same as for aileron.	
3. Elevator Flying Tab Check - same as for rudder except Art. Feel must be OFF before engaging Elev FT controls. Art. Feel ENG after performing check.	
4. Master switch OFF.	
5. Auto FT Power OFF, Inverter SMALL, and Gyro IN.	
6. Hyd Shutoff Valve Master switches OFF.	
7. Cyl Valve Mast switches OFF.	
	8. Hand pump system charging valves OFF (at hand pump accumulators on the flight deck).

PROPELLER VIBRATION RESTRICTIONS

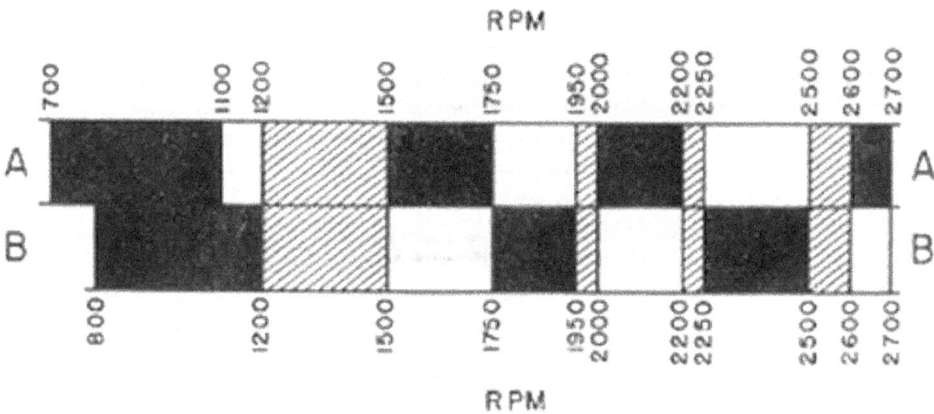

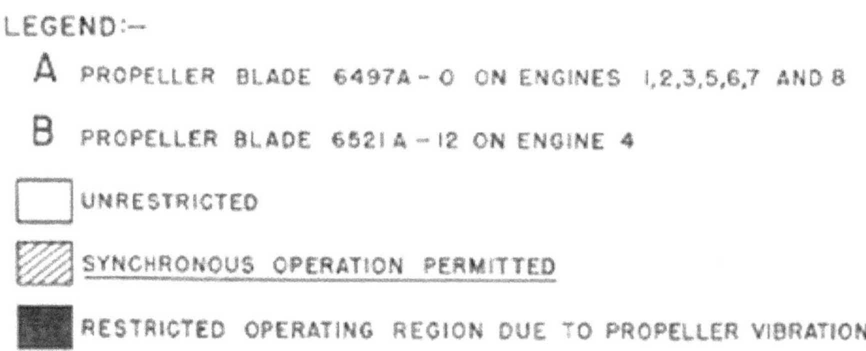

STALLING SPEEDS

POWER OFF

(ESTIMATED)

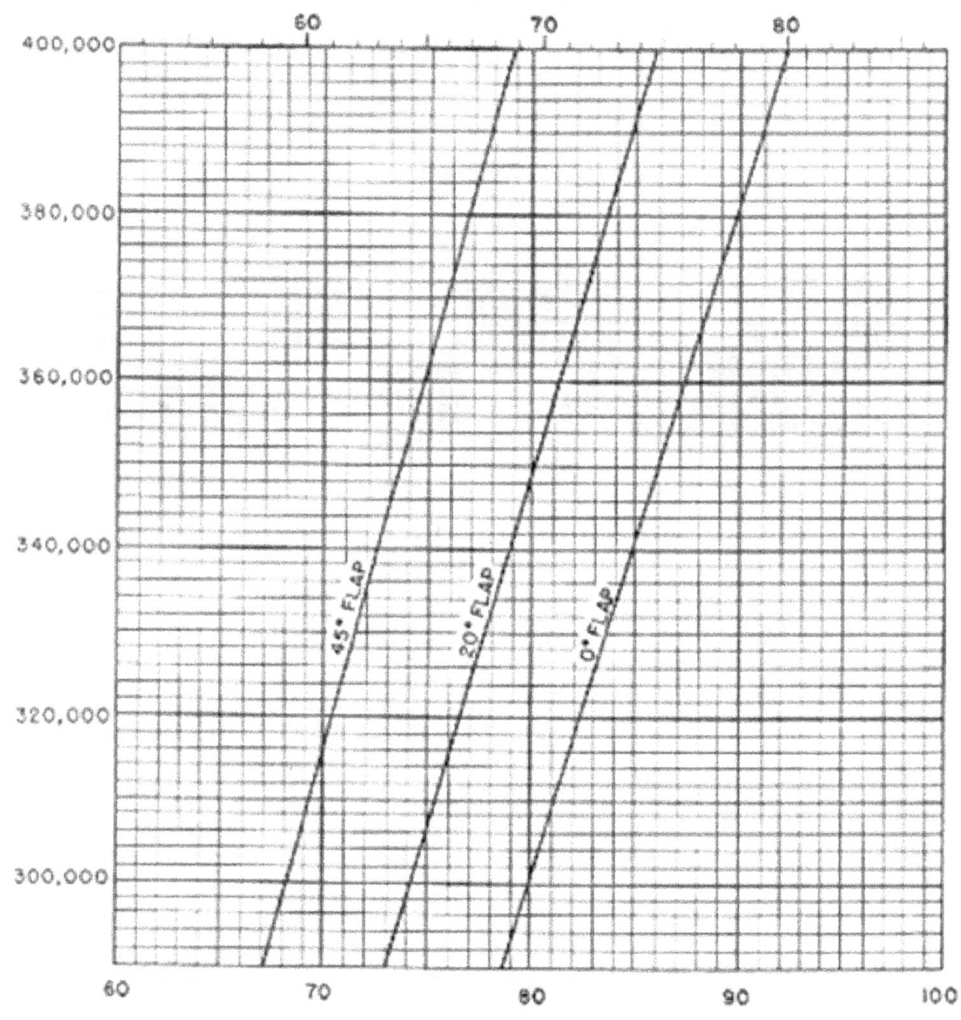

TAKEOFF TIME AND DISTANCE

2700 RPM 202 BMEP CG 29.5%

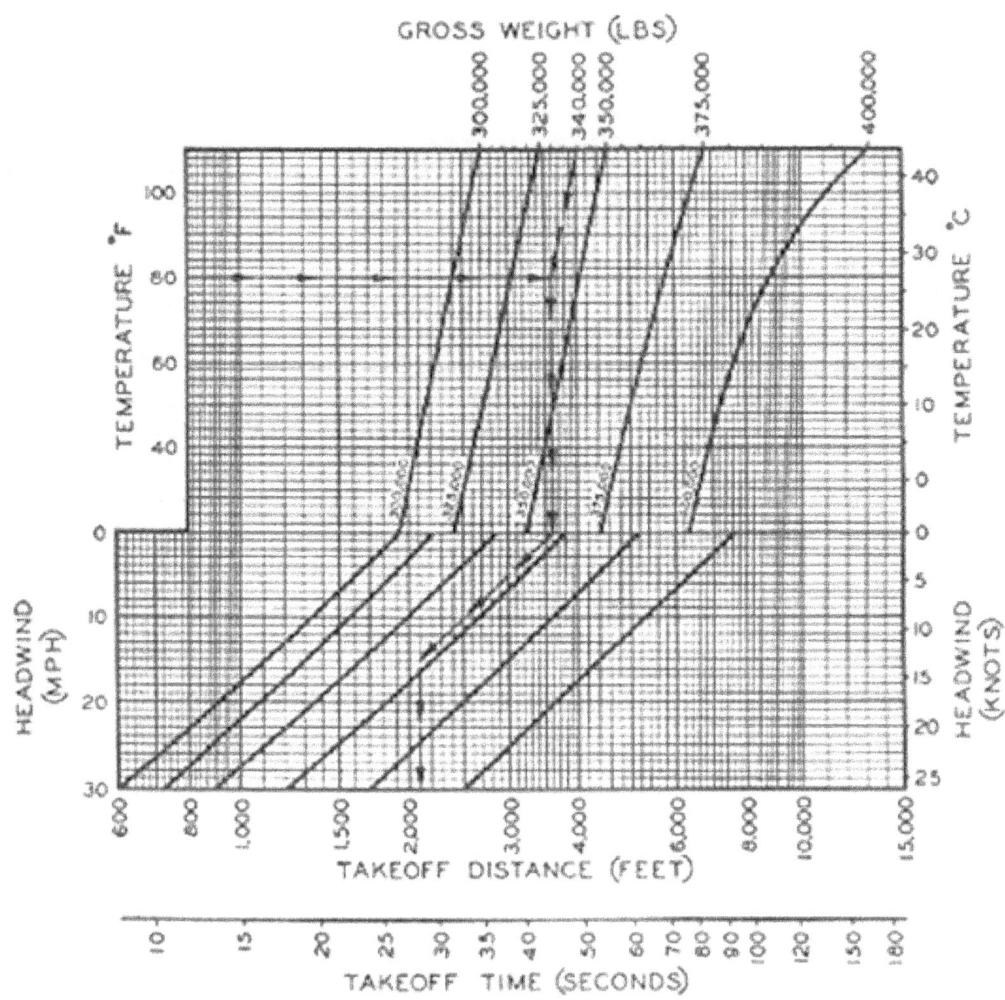

EXAMPLE:-
340000 LBS GROSS WT
80°F TEMPERATURE
15 MPH HEADWIND
FROM CHART:-
TAKEOFF DIST 2100 FT
TAKEOFF TIME 28.5 SEC

NOTE:
1. 20° FLAP DEFLECTION
2. 0° ELEVATOR DEFLECTION AT HUMP SPEED
3. PRELIMINARY - BASED BASED UPON POWER-OFF MODEL TESTS

TAKEOFF TIME AND DISTANCE

400,000 LBS GROSS WT

C G 29.5%   202 BMEP

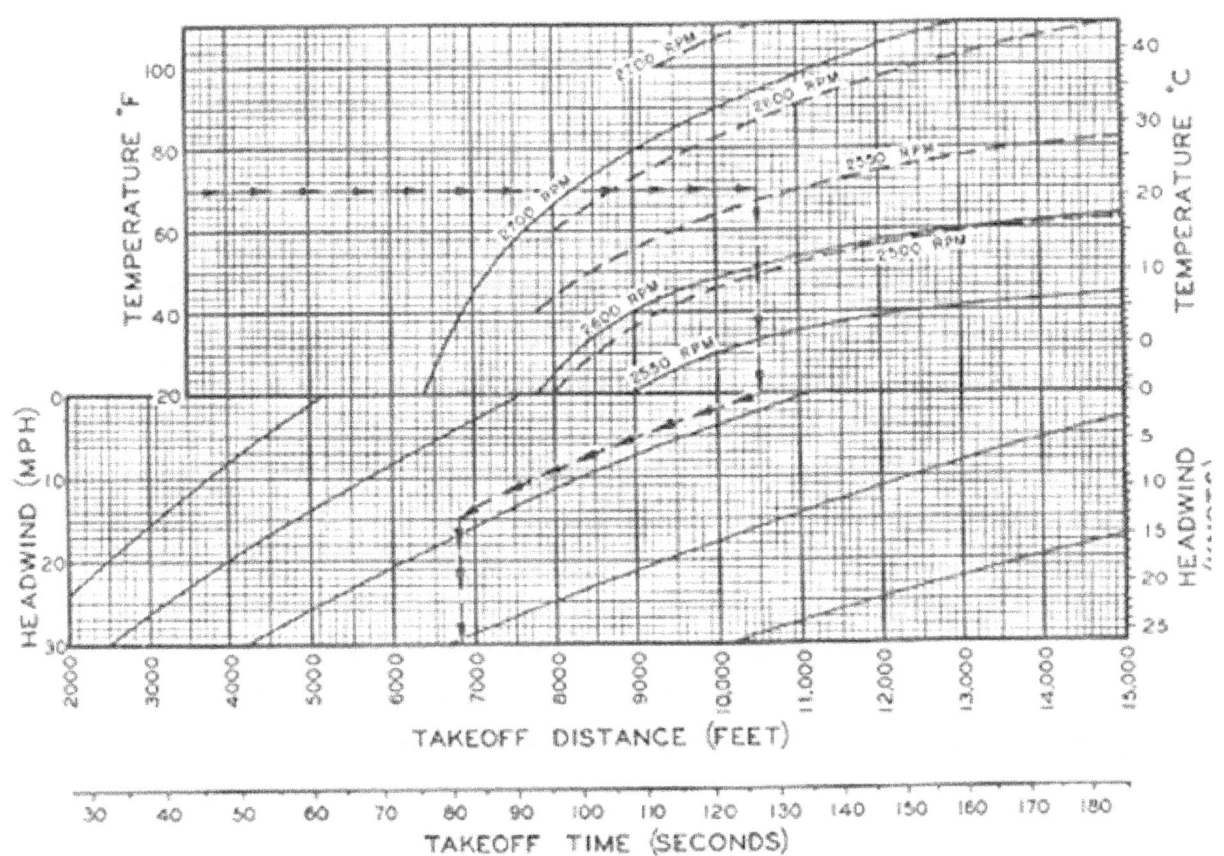

NOTES:-

1. — — — DASHED LINE +5° ELEVATOR DEFLECTION AT HUMP SPEED
2. ———— SOLID LINE 0° ELEVATOR DEFLECTION AT HUMP SPEED
3. PRELIMINARY-BASED UPON POWER-OFF MODEL TESTS
4. 20° FLAP DEFLECTION
5. OPERATION BETWEEN 2600 & 2700 RPM RESTRICTED DUE TO PROP VIBRATION

TAKEOFF TIME AND DISTANCE

350,000 LBS GROSS WT

CG 29.5 %   202 BMEP

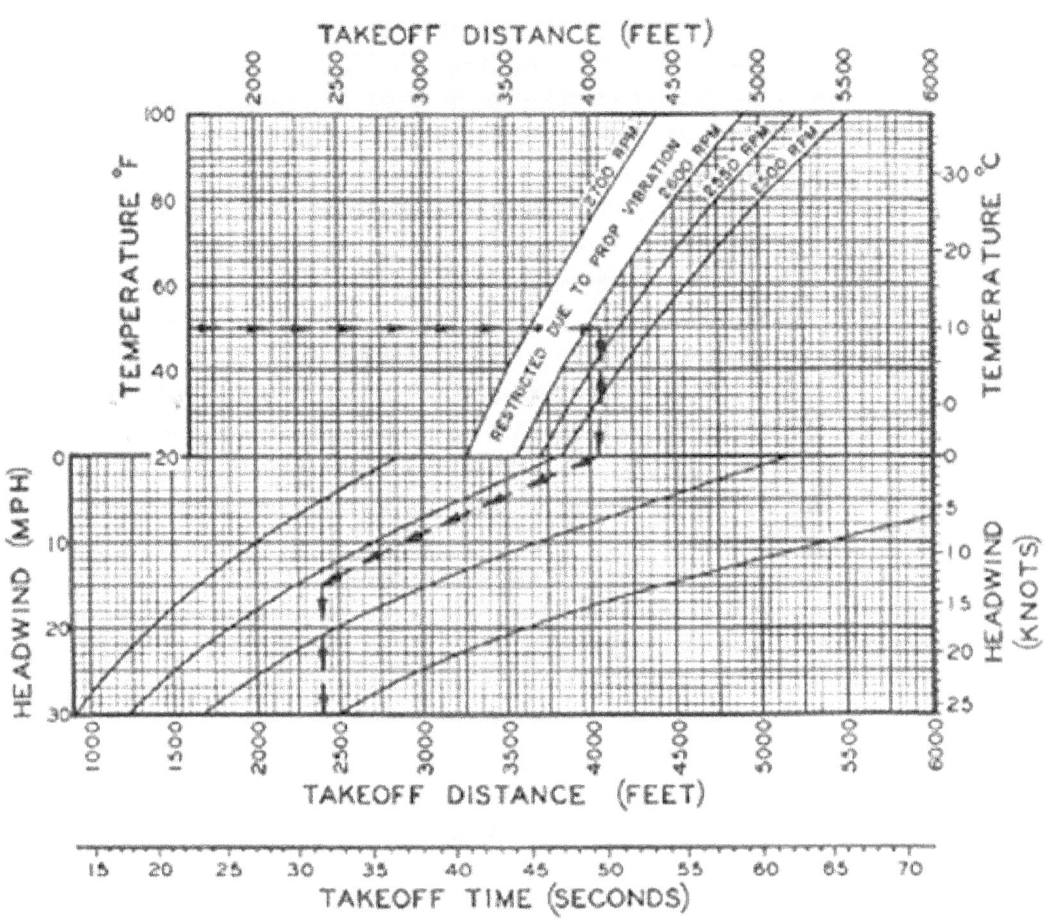

NOTES:—

1. 20° FLAP DEFLECTION
2. 0° ELEVATOR DEFLECTION AT HUMP SPEED
3. PRELIMINARY - BASED UPON POWER-OFF MODEL TESTS

TAKEOFF TRIM TRACK

350,000 LBS GROSS WT – CG 29.5%

WATER SPEED (KNOTS)

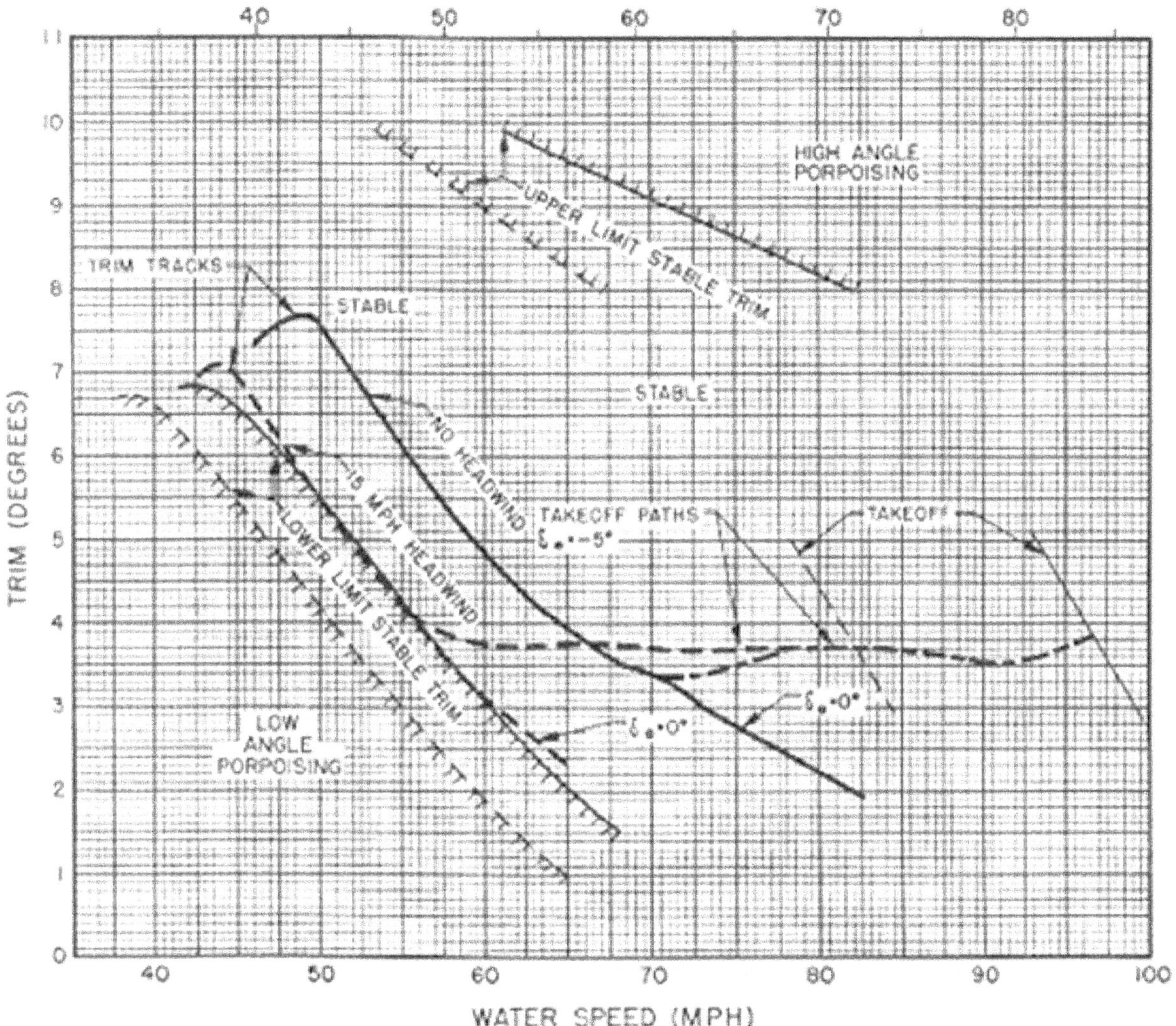

NOTES:

1. ——— SOLID LINE NO HEADWIND
2. – – – DASHED LINE 15 MPH HEADWIND
3. PRELIMINARY – BASED UPON POWER OFF MODEL TESTS
4. 20° FLAP DEFLECTION
5. TRIM ANGLE IS ANGLE BETWEEN UNDISTURBED WATER SURFACE AND HULL REFERENCE LINE

TAKEOFF TRIM TRACK

400,000 LBS GROSS WT C G 29.5%

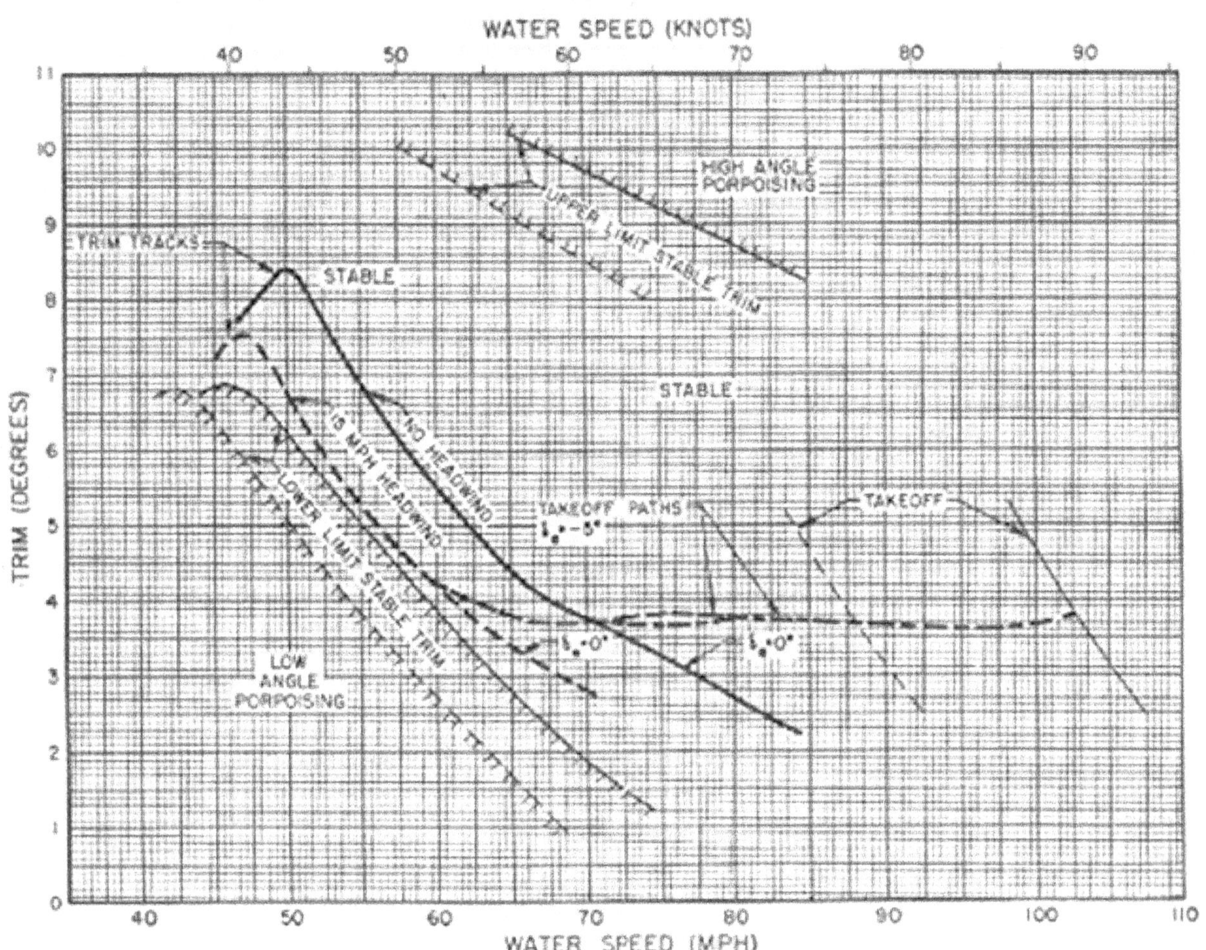

NOTES:

1 ——— SOLID LINE NO HEADWIND
2 — — — DASHED LINE 15 MPH HEADWIND
3 PRELIMINARY— BASED UPON POWER OFF MODEL TESTS
4 20° FLAP DEFLECTION
5 TRIM ANGLE IS ANGLE BETWEEN UNDISTURBED WATER SURFACE AND HULL REFERENCE LINE

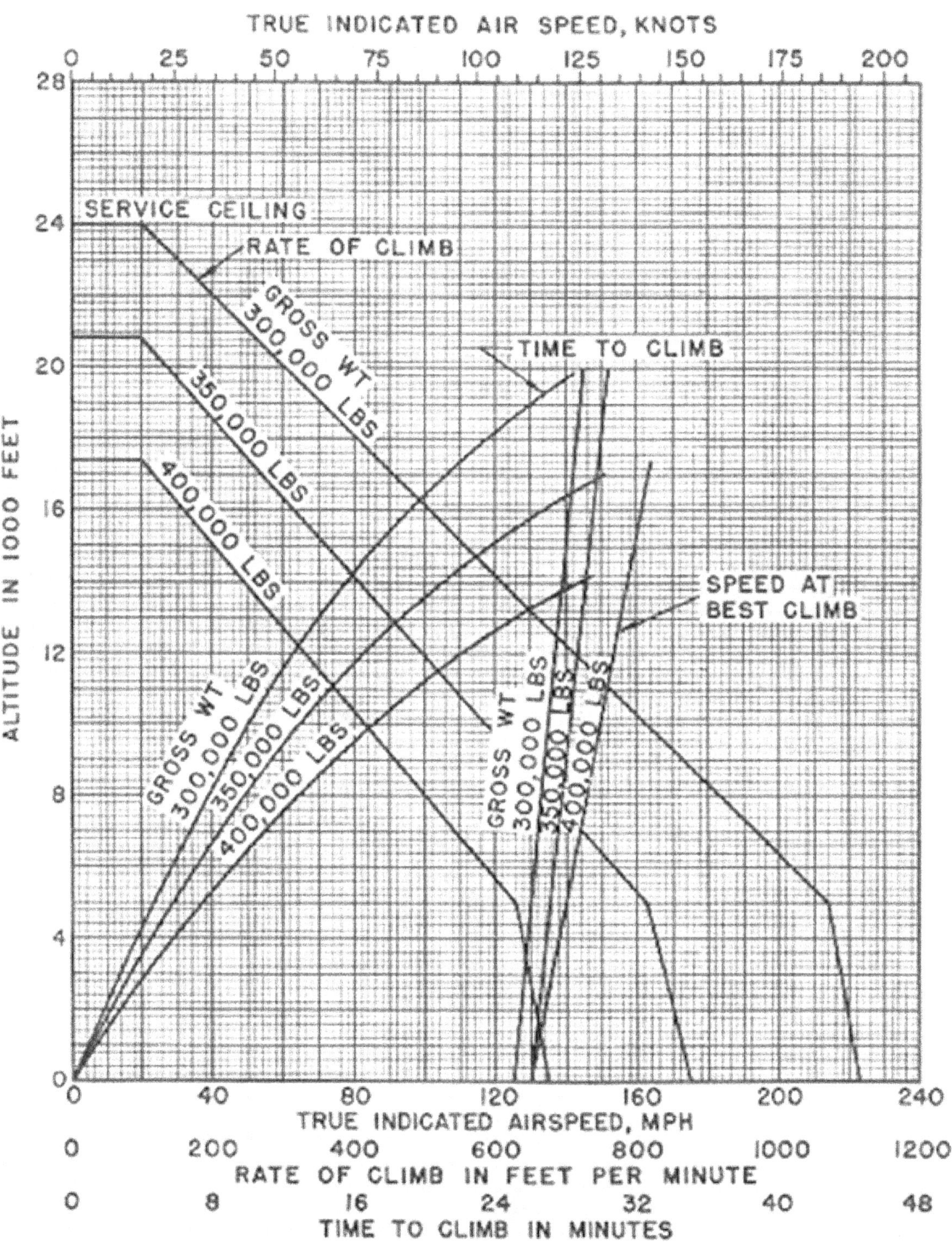
CLIMB DATA
NORMAL RATED POWER
(STD DAY)
TRUE INDICATED AIR SPEED, KNOTS
0
25
50
75
100
125
150
175
200
28
24
20
16
12
8
4
0
SERVICE CEILING
RATE OF CLIMB
GROSS WT 300,000 LBS
350,000 LBS
400,000 LBS
TIME TO CLIMB
SPEED AT BEST CLIMB
GROSS WT 300,000 LBS
350,000 LBS
400,000 LBS
GROSS WT 300,000 LBS
350,000 LBS
400,000 LBS
ALTITUDE IN 1000 FEET
0
40
80
120
160
200
240
TRUE INDICATED AIRSPEED, MPH
0
200
400
600
800
1000
1200
RATE OF CLIMB IN FEET PER MINUTE
0
8
16
24
32
40
48
TIME TO CLIMB IN MINUTES
NOTE:— PRELIMINARY-BASED UPON MODEL TEST DATA

B M E P POWER SETTINGS

HIGH POWER AUTO-RICH

P & W R4360-4A ENGINES

BRAKE MEAN EFFECTIVE PRESSURE (LBS/SQ IN.)

202 BMEP

RPM	ALT (FT)	Manifold Pressure at Carb Air Temp A	B	C	D	Fuel Flow LBS/HR	% Rated Power
[illegible]	[illegible]	[illegible]	[illegible]	[illegible]		[illegible]	[illegible]
[illegible]	[illegible]	[illegible]	[illegible]	[illegible]		[illegible]	[illegible]
[illegible]	[illegible]	[illegible]	[illegible]			[illegible]	[illegible]
[illegible]	[illegible]	[illegible]	[illegible]			[illegible]	[illegible]

193 BMEP

RPM	ALT (FT)	Manifold Pressure at Carb Air Temp A	B	C	D	Fuel Flow LBS/HR	% Rated Power
[illegible]	[illegible]	[illegible]	[illegible]	[illegible]	[illegible]	[illegible]	[illegible]
[illegible]	[illegible]	[illegible]	[illegible]	[illegible]		[illegible]	[illegible]
[illegible]	[illegible]	[illegible]	[illegible]	[illegible]		[illegible]	[illegible]
[illegible]	[illegible]	[illegible]	[illegible]	[illegible]		[illegible]	[illegible]

185 BMEP

RPM	ALT (FT)	Manifold Pressure at Carb Air Temp A	B	C	D	Fuel Flow LBS/HR	% Rated Power
[illegible]	[illegible]	[illegible]	[illegible]	[illegible]	[illegible]	[illegible]	[illegible]
[illegible]	[illegible]	[illegible]	[illegible]	[illegible]	[illegible]	[illegible]	[illegible]
[illegible]	[illegible]	[illegible]	[illegible]	[illegible]	[illegible]	[illegible]	[illegible]
[illegible]	[illegible]	[illegible]	[illegible]	[illegible]	[illegible]	[illegible]	[illegible]

178 BMEP

RPM	ALT (FT)	Manifold Pressure at Carb Air Temp A	B	C	D	Fuel Flow LBS/HR	% Rated Power
[illegible]	[illegible]	[illegible]	[illegible]	[illegible]	[illegible]	[illegible]	[illegible]
[illegible]	[illegible]	[illegible]	[illegible]	[illegible]	[illegible]	[illegible]	[illegible]
[illegible]	[illegible]	[illegible]	[illegible]	[illegible]	[illegible]	[illegible]	[illegible]
[illegible]	[illegible]	[illegible]	[illegible]	[illegible]	[illegible]	[illegible]	[illegible]
[illegible]	[illegible]	[illegible]	[illegible]	[illegible]	[illegible]	[illegible]	[illegible]
[illegible]	[illegible]	[illegible]	[illegible]	[illegible]	[illegible]	[illegible]	[illegible]
[illegible]	[illegible]	[illegible]	[illegible]	[illegible]	[illegible]	[illegible]	[illegible]
[illegible]	[illegible]	[illegible]	[illegible]	[illegible]	[illegible]	[illegible]	[illegible]
[illegible]	[illegible]	[illegible]	[illegible]	[illegible]	[illegible]	[illegible]	[illegible]

165 BMEP

RPM	ALT (FT)	Manifold Pressure at Carb Air Temp A	B	C	D	Fuel Flow LBS/HR	% Rated Power
[illegible]	[illegible]	[illegible]	[illegible]	[illegible]	[illegible]	[illegible]	[illegible]
[illegible]	[illegible]	[illegible]	[illegible]	[illegible]	[illegible]	[illegible]	[illegible]
[illegible]	[illegible]	[illegible]	[illegible]	[illegible]	[illegible]	[illegible]	[illegible]
[illegible]	[illegible]	[illegible]	[illegible]	[illegible]	[illegible]	[illegible]	[illegible]
[illegible]	[illegible]	[illegible]	[illegible]	[illegible]	[illegible]	[illegible]	[illegible]
[illegible]	[illegible]	[illegible]	[illegible]	[illegible]	[illegible]	[illegible]	[illegible]
[illegible]	[illegible]	[illegible]	[illegible]	[illegible]	[illegible]	[illegible]	[illegible]
[illegible]	[illegible]	[illegible]	[illegible]	[illegible]	[illegible]	[illegible]	[illegible]
[illegible]	[illegible]	[illegible]	[illegible]	[illegible]	[illegible]	[illegible]	[illegible]

150 BMEP

RPM	ALT (FT)	Manifold Pressure at Carb Air Temp A	B	C	D	Fuel Flow LBS/HR	% Rated Power
[illegible]	[illegible]	[illegible]	[illegible]	[illegible]	[illegible]	[illegible]	[illegible]
[illegible]	[illegible]	[illegible]	[illegible]	[illegible]	[illegible]	[illegible]	[illegible]
[illegible]	[illegible]	[illegible]	[illegible]	[illegible]	[illegible]	[illegible]	[illegible]
[illegible]	[illegible]	[illegible]	[illegible]	[illegible]	[illegible]	[illegible]	[illegible]
[illegible]	[illegible]	[illegible]	[illegible]	[illegible]	[illegible]	[illegible]	[illegible]
[illegible]	[illegible]	[illegible]	[illegible]	[illegible]	[illegible]	[illegible]	[illegible]
[illegible]	[illegible]	[illegible]	[illegible]	[illegible]	[illegible]	[illegible]	[illegible]
[illegible]	[illegible]	[illegible]	[illegible]	[illegible]	[illegible]	[illegible]	[illegible]
[illegible]	[illegible]	[illegible]	[illegible]	[illegible]	[illegible]	[illegible]	[illegible]

NOTE

1. [illegible]
2. [illegible]
3. [illegible]
4. [illegible]
5. FUEL FLOW [illegible]
6. % RATED POWER [illegible]
7. [illegible]

ALT (FT)	A	B	C	D
[illegible]	[illegible]	[illegible]	[illegible]	[illegible]

HIGH POWER AUTO-RICH

LOW POWER AUTO RICH

B M E P POWER SETTINGS

LOW POWER AUTO-RICH

P & W R4360-4A ENGINES

BRAKE MEAN EFFECTIVE PRESSURE (LBS/SQ IN.)

150 BMEP*

RPM	ALT (FT)	Manifold Pressure at Carb Air Temp A	B	C	D	Fuel Flow (LB/HR)	Rated Power (%)
1950	S.L. 5,000 8,300	33.0 32.3 31.3	34.6 33.6 32.6	34.5 33.5	35.4 34.3	758 686	60% 1600
1900	S.L. 5,000 8,300	32.8 31.8 31.2	33.6 32.8 32.1	34.3 33.3	35.2 34.1	784 712	63% 1575
1850	S.L. 5,000 7,800	32.6 31.5 31.0	33.6 32.5 32.5	34.1 33.2	34.9 33.8	756 687	61% 1525
1800	S.L. 5,000 7,600	32.5 31.3 30.8	33.5 32.3 31.0	34.0 32.8	34.8 33.6	723 655	59% 1475
1500	S.L. 4,500	31.8 30.7	32.8 31.6	33.3	34.1	592 536	50% 1250
1450	S.L. 3,800	31.7 30.3	32.7 31.6	33.2	34.0	573 519	48% 1200
1400	S.L. 3,400	31.5 30.6	32.5 31.5	33.0	33.8	555 503	46% 1150

140 BMEP*

RPM	ALT (FT)	Manifold Pressure at Carb Air Temp A	B	C	D	Fuel Flow (LB/HR)	Rated Power (%)
1950	S.L. 5,000 8,000 11,325	31.3 30.4 29.4 27.3	32.3 31.3 30.3 30.2	32.8 31.8	33.6 32.6	758 684	60% 1500
1900	S.L. 5,000 10,000 10,150	31.2 30.3 29.1 29.1	32.2 31.2 31.2 31.0	32.7 31.7	33.5 32.6	731 661	59% 1475
1850	S.L. 5,000 9,895	31.0 30.1 28.9	32.0 31.0 29.8	32.5 31.5	33.3 32.2	708	57% 1425
1800	S.L. 5,000 9,300	30.8 29.8 28.9	31.8 30.7 29.6	32.3 31.2	33.1 31.6	686 620	56% 1400
1500	S.L. 5,000 7,900	30.3 28.9 29.3	31.3 29.8 29.2	31.7 30.2	32.4	563 509	46% 1150
1450	S.L. 5,000 6,600	30.2 28.7 28.3	31.2 29.6 29.2	31.6	32.3	546 494	45% 1125
1400	S.L. 5,000 6,000	30.1 28.7 28.5	31.0 29.6 29.2	31.4	32.2	528 478	43% 1075

130 BMEP*

RPM	ALT (FT)	Manifold Pressure at Carb Air Temp A	B	C	D	Fuel Flow (LB/HR)	Rated Power (%)
1950	S.L. 5,000 10,000 12,000	29.8 28.7 27.7 27.7	30.7 29.6 28.6 28.1	31.2 30.2 28.1	31.9 30.8 29.7	689 642	56% 1400
1900	S.L. 5,000 10,000 13,000	29.6 28.5 27.5 27.2	30.5 29.4 28.4 28.0	31.0 29.9 28.7	31.7 30.6	699 623	54% 1350
1850	S.L. 5,000 10,000 11,700	29.5 28.4 27.4 27.2	30.4 29.3 28.2 27.6	30.9 29.7 28.5	31.6 30.5	614 564	53% 1325
1800	S.L. 5,000 10,000 11,100	29.3 28.2 27.2 27.0	30.2 29.1 28.0 27.6	30.7 29.3	31.4 32.3	647 585	52% 1300
1500	S.L. 5,000 10,300	28.6 27.5 25.7	29.5 28.1 26.5	29.9 28.6	30.7 29.2	531 481	43% 1075
1450	S.L. 5,000 9,400	28.3 27.0 25.7	29.4 27.8 26.5	28.8 28.2	30.1	518 463	42% 1050
1400	S.L. 5,000 9,000	28.4 27.0 25.9	29.1 27.8 26.5	29.7 28.1	30.5	504 452	40% 1000

120 BMEP*

RPM	ALT (FT)	Manifold Pressure at Carb Air Temp A	B	C	D	Fuel Flow (LB/HR)	Rated Power (%)
1950	S.L. 5,000 10,200 14,800	28.2 27.1 26.1 25.0	29.1 27.9 26.9 25.8	29.5 28.3 27.3	30.1 29.0 28.2	664 608	52% 1300
1900	S.L. 5,000 10,000 14,500	28.0 26.6 26.0 24.5	28.9 27.9 26.8 25.7	29.3 28.5 27.3	30.2 28.7 27.9	644 582	50% 1250
1850	S.L. 5,000 10,200 14,500	27.8 26.7 25.8 24.7	28.7 27.6 26.6 25.5	29.1 27.9 27.0	29.8 28.6 27.7	626 566	49% 1225
1800	S.L. 5,000 10,000 12,500	27.6 26.7 25.6 24.7	28.5 27.5 26.4 25.5	28.9 27.8 26.8	29.5 28.6 27.5	626 568	48% 1200
1500	S.L. 5,000 10,000 13,000	27.1 25.4 24.1 23.4	27.9 26.2 25.1 24.2	28.3 26.6	29.0 27.3	502 455	41% 1025
1450	S.L. 5,000 10,000 12,700	27.3 25.9 25.1 23.3	27.6 26.2 24.9 24.0	28.2 26.6	28.7	487 441	38% 950
1400	S.L. 5,000 10,000 12,300	26.9 25.6 23.9 23.2	27.7 26.2 25.6 23.9	28.1 26.5	28.8	471 427	37% 925

NOTE:

1. Altitudes shown are carburetor top deck pressure altitudes.
2. The following carburetor air temperatures apply to these columns:

ALT (FT)	A	B	C	D
S.L.	30°F	60°F	75°F	100°F
5,000	12°	42°	57°	82°
10,000	-6°	24°	39°	64°
15,000	-23°	7°	22°	47°

3. Avoid operating in the following restricted ranges: 100-1200 rpm, 1550-1750 rpm, 2000-2200 rpm, above 2600 rpm.
4. (*) On engines operating with accessory drive, reduce BMEP settings by 2 psi.
5. "FUEL FLOW" column indicates probable range of fuel flows for particular power setting.
6. "RATED POWER" column lists percentage of the normal rated power.
7. (------) Altitudes underlined with a dashed line represent critical carburetor top deck pressure altitudes on a standard day.

B M E P POWER SETTINGS

AUTO-LEAN CRUISE

P&W R4360-4A ENGINES

BRAKE MEAN EFFECTIVE PRESSURE (LBS/SQ IN.)

150 BMEP*

RPM	ALT (FT)	MANIFOLD PRESSURE AT CARB AIR TEMP A	B	C	D	FUEL FLOW (LBS/HR)	RATED POWER (%)
1950	S.L. 5,000 6,250	35.1 34.1 33.8	36.2 35.2 34.8	36.7 35.7	37.6	725 656	65% 1600
1900	S.L. 5,000 5,800	35.0 34.0 33.8	36.1 35.0 34.8	36.6 35.5	37.5	704 639	63% 1575
1850	S.L. 5,000 5,600	34.8 33.5 33.4	35.9 34.5 34.4	36.4	37.3	684 618	61% 1525
1800	S.L. 5,000 5,250	34.6 33.5 33.2	35.7 34.3 34.2	36.2	37.1	660 598	59% 1475
1500	S.L. 3,400	32.2 32.2	34.2 33.2	34.7	35.6	538	50% 1250
1450	S.L. 3,250	33.1 32.1	34.1 33.1	34.6	35.5	519 469	48% 1200
1400	S.L. 2,800	33.0 32.1	34.0 33.1	34.8	35.4	488 450	46% 1150

143 BMEP*

RPM	ALT (FT)	MANIFOLD PRESSURE AT CARB AIR TEMP A	B	C	D	FUEL FLOW (LBS/HR)	RATED POWER (%)
1950	S.L. 5,000 7,030	33.4 32.4 31.9	34.6 33.4 32.9	35.1 33.9	36.8 34.7	685 619	60% 1500
1900	S.L. 5,000 7,500	33.3 32.2 32.7	34.3 33.2 32.7	34.8 33.7	35.7 34.5	665 601	59% 1475
1850	S.L. 5,000 7,300	33.1 31.8 31.5	34.1 32.8 32.5	34.6 33.1	35.5 34.1	645 585	57% 1425
1800	S.L. 5,000 7,100	32.8 31.5 31.1	33.8 32.5 32.1	34.3 33.0	36.2 35.8	624 564	56% 1400
1500	S.L. 5,000 5,300	31.9 32.2 32.1	32.9 31.5 31.0	33.0	33.8	546 459	46% 1150
1450	S.L. 5,000 5,200	31.4 30.1 30.1	32.4 31.0 31.0	32.9	33.7	487 441	45% 1125
1400	S.L. 4,600	31.4 30.1	32.4 31.0	32.9	33.7	468 424	43% 1075

133 BMEP*

RPM	ALT (FT)	MANIFOLD PRESSURE AT CARB AIR TEMP A	B	C	D	FUEL FLOW (LBS/HR)	RATED POWER (%)
1950	S.L. 5,000 5,600	31.8 30.7 29.6	32.8 31.6 31.5	33.3 32.1	34.1 32.9	646 584	56% 1400
1900	S.L. 5,000 5,600	31.6 30.4 29.5	32.6 31.3 30.4	33.1 31.8	33.9 32.6	626 566	54% 1350
1850	S.L. 5,000 5,320	31.4 30.2 29.3	32.4 31.1 30.2	32.9 31.8	33.7 32.5	607 549	53% 1325
1800	S.L. 5,000 5,100	31.1 29.9 29.1	32.1 30.8 30.6	32.6 31.3	33.4 32.0	585 529	52% 1300
1500	S.L. 5,000 7,600	29.9 28.6 27.9	30.8 29.5 28.8	31.3 29.9	32.0 30.7	475 429	43% 1075
1450	S.L. 5,000 7,300	29.9 28.5 27.9	30.8 29.4 28.8	31.3 29.8	32.0 30.6	457 413	42% 1050
1400	S.L. 5,000 7,000	29.9 28.4 27.9	30.8 29.3 28.8	31.3 29.7	32.0 30.5	440 398	40% 1000

127 BMEP*

RPM	ALT (FT)	MANIFOLD PRESSURE AT CARB AIR TEMP A	B	C	D	FUEL FLOW (LBS/HR)	RATED POWER (%)
1950	S.L. 5,000 11,000 12,200	30.0 28.6 27.8 27.4	30.9 29.7 28.7 28.2	31.4 30.3 29.1	32.1 30.9 29.8	606 548	52% 1300
1900	S.L. 5,000 10,000 11,000	29.7 28.5 27.5 27.2	30.6 29.4 28.4 28.0	31.1 29.8 28.8	31.8 30.6	586 530	50% 1250
1850	S.L. 5,000 10,000 11,600	29.6 28.3 27.4 27.1	30.5 29.5 28.3 27.9	31.0 29.6 28.6	31.7 30.4	568 514	49% 1225
1800	S.L. 5,000 10,000 11,600	29.4 28.1 27.3 27.0	30.3 29.0 27.9 27.8	30.8 29.4 28.9	31.5 30.2	547 495	48% 1200
1500	S.L. 5,000 10,000	28.2 26.9 25.8	29.1 27.7 26.6	29.5 28.1	30.1 28.6	444 402	40% 1000
1450	S.L. 5,000 9,750	28.3 27.3 25.4	29.2 27.8 26.4	29.6 28.2	30.4 28.9	427 387	38% 950
1400	S.L. 5,000 9,400	28.3 27.1 25.9	29.2 27.9 26.7	30.6 28.9	30.4 29.0	412 372	37% 925

NOTE:-

1. Altitudes shown are carburetor top deck pressure altitudes.
2. The following carburetor air temperatures apply to these columns:

ALT (FT)	A	B	C	D
S.L.	30°F	68°F	75°F	100°F
5,000	12°	47°	57°	82°
10,000	-4°	26°	39°	64°
15,000	-23°	7°	22°	47°

3. Avoid operating in the following restricted ranges: [illegible] rpm, 1550-1750 rpm, 2000-2200 rpm, above 2600 rpm.
4. (*) On engines operating with accessory loads, reduce BMEP settings by 2 psi.
5. "FUEL FLOW" column indicates probable range of fuel flows for particular power setting.
6. "RATED POWER" column lists percentage of the normal rated power.
7. (------) Altitudes underlined with a dashed line represent critical carburetor top deck pressure altitudes on a standard day.

AUTO-LEAN CRUISE

AUTO-LEAN CRUISE

DENSITY ALTITUDE CHART

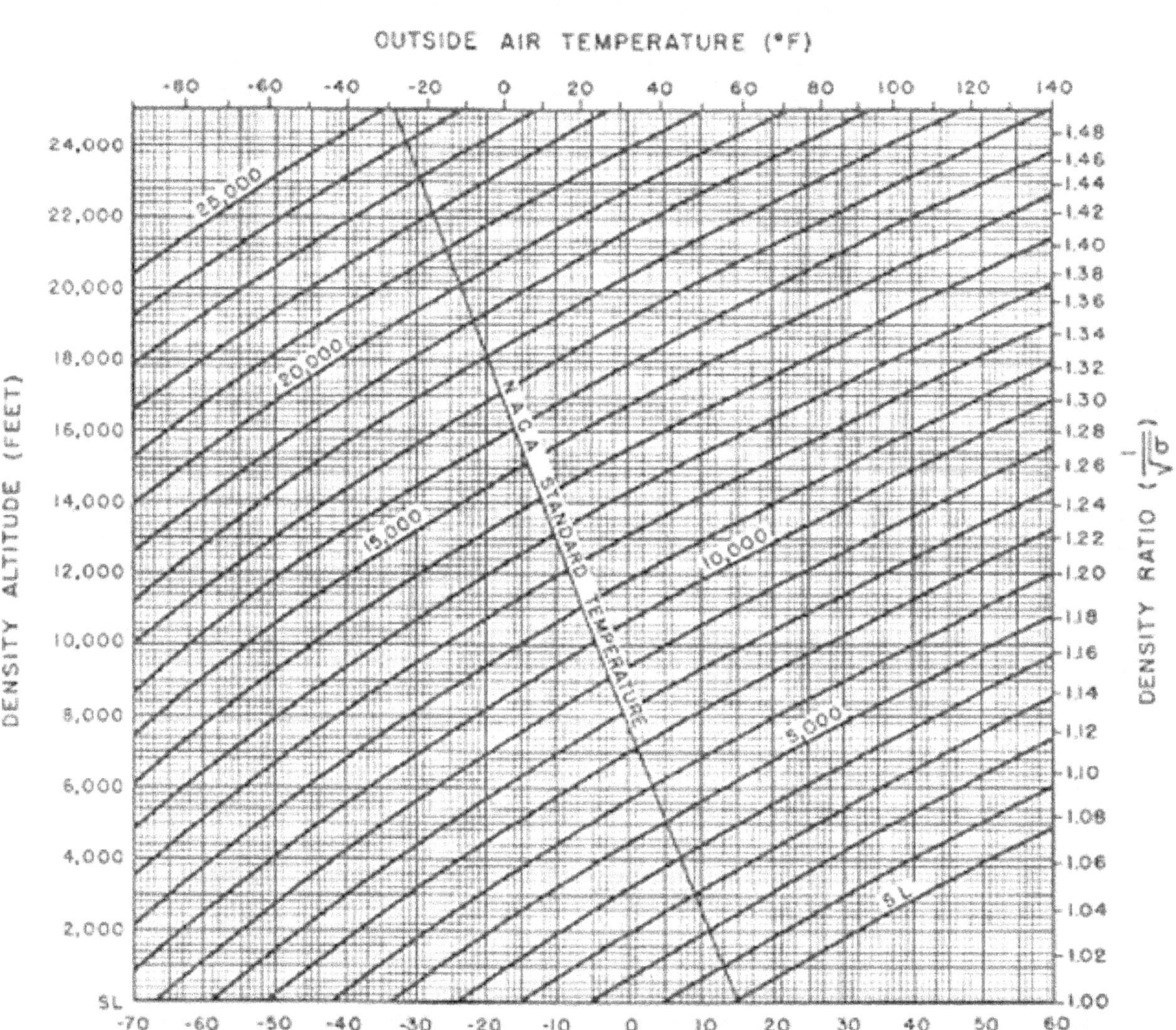

AIRSPEED CONVERSION CHART

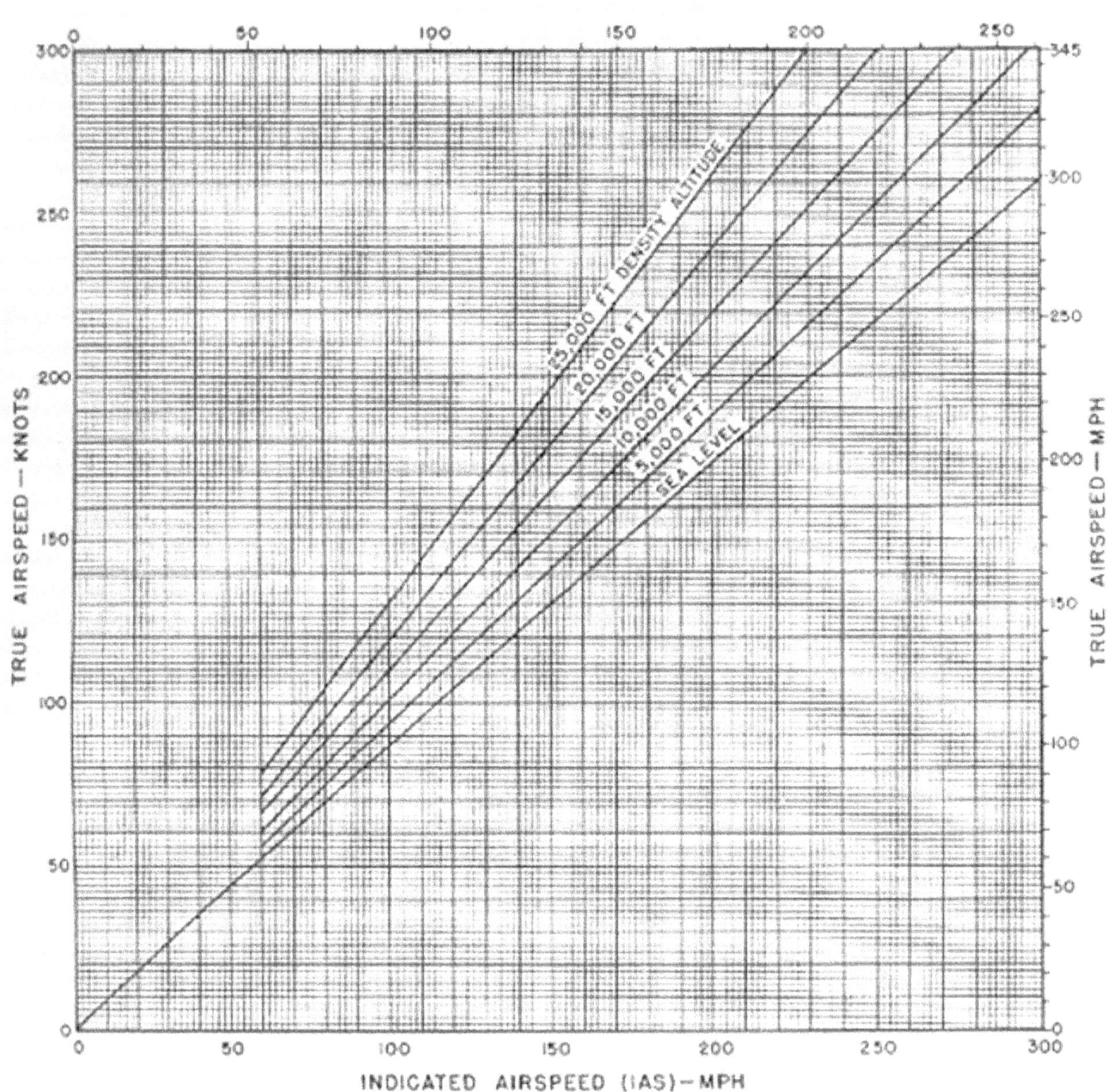

NOTE:—
100 KNOTS=115 MPH

CARBURETOR AIR TEMPERATURE CORRECTIONS

MANIFOLD PRESSURE

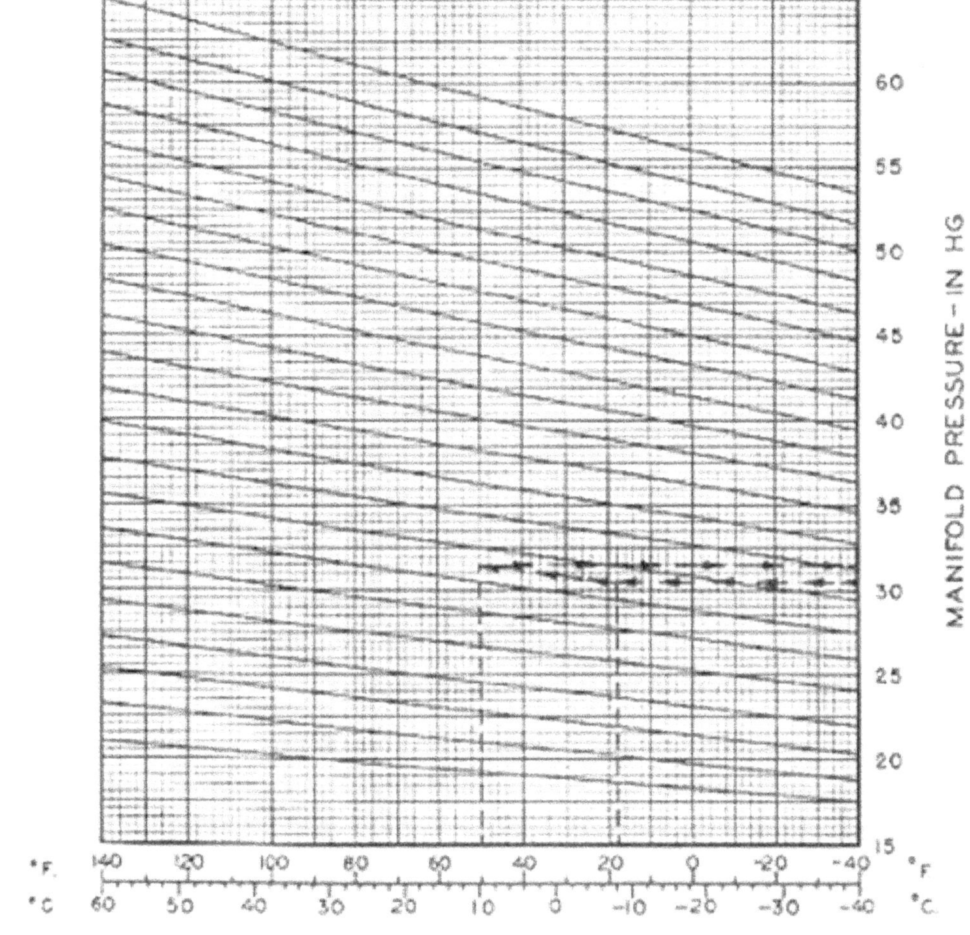

CARBURETOR AIR TEMPERATURE DEGREES

USE:—

TO CORRECT MANIFOLD PRESSURE READINGS OBTAINED FROM STANDARD TEMPERATURE ENGINE CALIBRATION CHART.

EXAMPLE:—

MANIFOLD PRESSURE CORRECTION—USING AUTO RICH STANDARD TEMPERATURE ENGINE CALIBRATION CHART EXAMPLE AND ASSUMING 50°F CARBURETOR AIR TEMPERATURE, ENTER TEMPERATURE CORRECTION CHART AT MANIFOLD PRESSURE (30.5 IN. HG.), FOLLOW LINE HORIZONTALLY TO STANDARD ALTITUDE TEMPERATURE (19°F), THEN PARALLEL SLANT LINE TO 50°F CARBURETOR AIR TEMPERATURE. READ HORIZONTALLY FROM INTERSECTION, CORRECTED MANIFOLD PRESSURE (31.5 IN. HG).

TEMPERATURE CONVERSION CHART

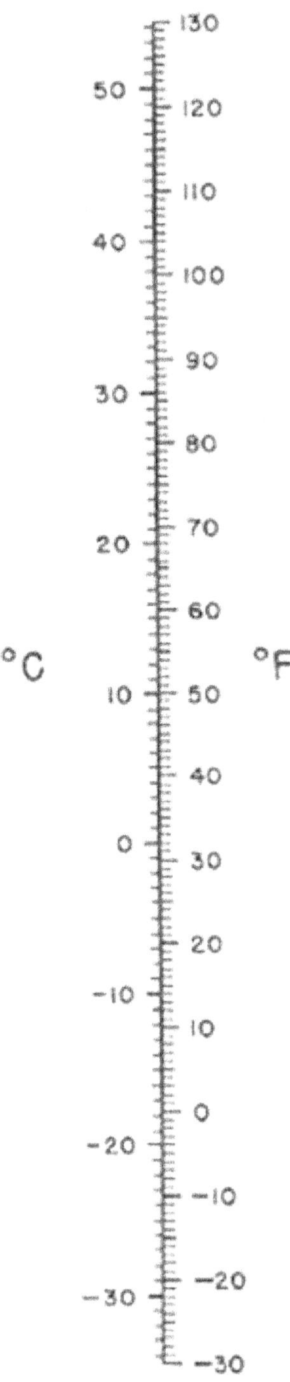

AIRCRAFT AT WAR DVD SERIES

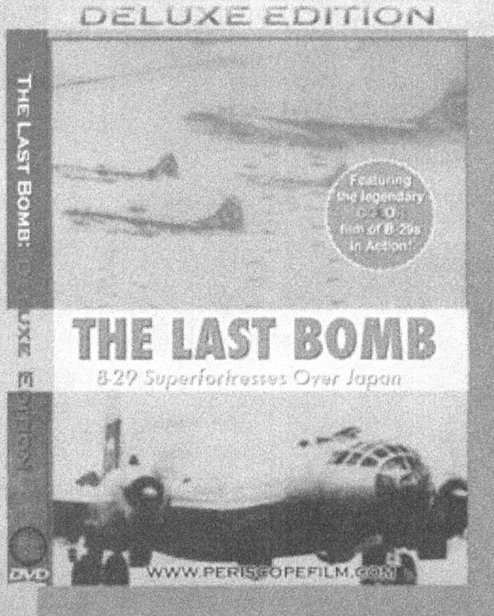

NOW AVAILABLE!

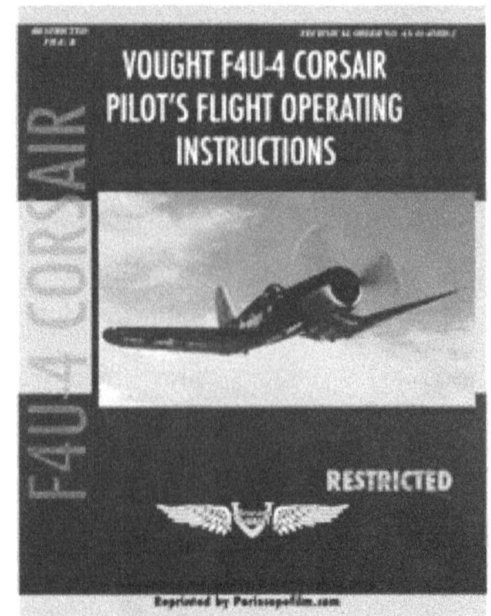
VOUGHT F4U-4 CORSAIR
PILOT'S FLIGHT OPERATING
INSTRUCTIONS
F4U-4 CORSAIR
RESTRICTED
Reprinted by Periscopefilm.com

THE FLEET TYPE
SUBMARINE
The definitive technical guide – profiling the submarines of World War II
RESTRICTED
Originally published as NAVPERS 16160
June 1946
WWW.PERISCOPEFILM.COM

CURTISS P-40 WARHAWK
PILOT'S FLIGHT OPERATING
MANUAL
FLYING TIGERS
RESTRICTED
Originally Published by the U.S. Army Air Force
Reprinted by Periscopefilm.com

NORTH AMERICAN X-15 ROCKET PLANE
PILOT'S FLIGHT OPERATING
INSTRUCTIONS
X-15 ROCKET PLANE
RESTRICTED
X-15
Originally Published by North American Aviation and the USAF
Reprinted by Periscopefilm.com

NORTHROP P-61 BLACK WIDOW
PILOT'S FLIGHT OPERATING
INSTRUCTIONS
NIGHT FIGHTER
RESTRICTED
Originally Published by USAAF July 1945
Reprinted by Periscopefilm.com

NORTHROP YB-49 FLYING WING
PILOT'S FLIGHT OPERATING
INSTRUCTIONS
FLYING WING
RESTRICTED
Reprinted by Periscopefilm.com

NORTH AMERICAN P-51 MUSTANG
PILOT'S FLIGHT OPERATING
INSTRUCTIONS
P-51 MUSTANG
RESTRICTED

B-17F
AIRPLANE
PILOT'S FLIGHT OPERATING
INSTRUCTIONS
B-17F
AIRPLANE
Originally published by the
United States Army Air Forces
December, 1942.
RESTRICTED

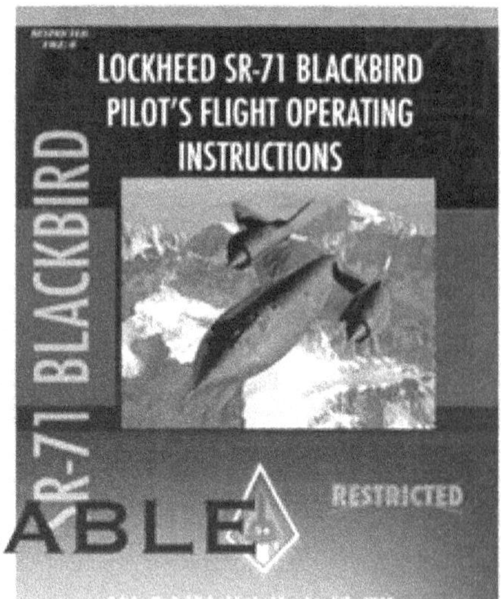
LOCKHEED SR-71 BLACKBIRD
PILOT'S FLIGHT OPERATING
INSTRUCTIONS
SR-71 BLACKBIRD
RESTRICTED
Originally Published by Lockheed and the USAF

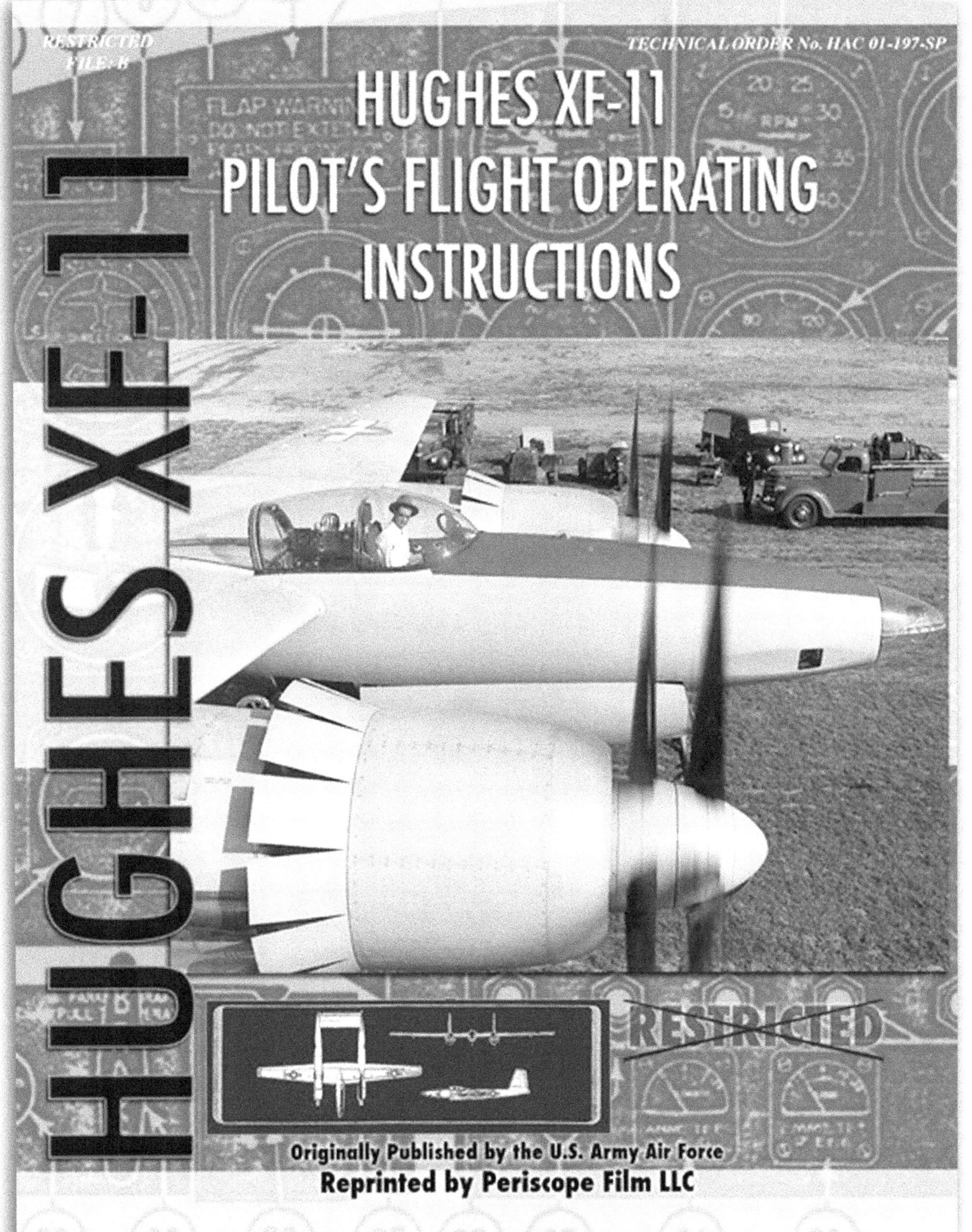
RESTRICTED
FILE: B
TECHNICAL ORDER No. HAC 01-197-SP
HUGHES XF-11
PILOT'S FLIGHT OPERATING
INSTRUCTIONS
HUGHES XF-11
RESTRICTED
Originally Published by the U.S. Army Air Force
Reprinted by Periscope Film LLC

ISBN #978-1-935327-78-3 1-935327-78-X

www.ingramcontent.com/pod-product-compliance
Lightning Source LLC
Chambersburg PA
CBHW080508110426
42742CB00017B/3032

* 9 7 8 1 9 3 5 3 2 7 7 8 3 *